D1539043

EDUCATION FOR LIVING

—Photo by Kathy Wersen

EDUCATION FOR LIVING

by

Jacob Samuel List, Ph.D., D.H.L.

GREENWOOD PRESS, PUBLISHERS
WESTPORT, CONNECTICUT

The Library of Congress has catalogued this publication as follows:

Library of Congress Cataloging in Publication Data

List, Jacob Samuel.
  Education for living.

  1. Psychotherapy.   I.   Title.
[RC480.5.L567   1972]   616.8'914   726200
ISBN 0-8371-6462-1

Originally published in 1961
by Philosophical Library, New York

Reprinted with the permission
of Dr. Davida List

First Greenwood Reprinting 1972

Library of Congress Catalogue Card Number 72-6200

ISBN 0-8371-6462-1

Printed in the United States of America

To my wife, Helen

TABLE OF CONTENTS

THE MAN BEHIND THE METHOD

This is a book about people, ordinary people like your friends and mine. If the word psychotherapy has brought to your mind a picture of patients lying upon a couch recalling childhood experiences, put this image aside. You will find no "patients" here, but pleasant people who are dissatisfied with their present way of living. They face the same problems that we all encounter in our daily lives, but have become aware that somehow they are putting obstacles in their own path. The List Method is the way in which one man has set about teaching people how to remove or avoid these obstacles, and how to get the most out of their lives. It is the therapeutic use of love, based upon understanding and respect, and teaches that the art of loving is the key to the art of living.

Jacob Samuel List is not a psychologist. He is an

educator and a philosopher, whose experiences have convinced him that nearly all our problems are the result of an unbalanced upbringing, in which attention has been too closely focused upon the child's intellectual development, at the expense of his emotional growth. Although modern educational methods are beginning to stress the importance of emotional factors, there is no institution in our society which assumes the full responsibility for the emotional education of our children. The schools are but one part of the child's life, and because of their role in our current society, are bound to regard emotional and spiritual education as subordinate to their prime function of training the intellect.

The churches should be a fount of wisdom from which a child could learn to understand (at his own level) the human elements of each situation he encounters, and to handle the emotions that arise from it. But congregations have dwindled because the churches cling to many outdated values, and too many of those people who continue to attend church give only lip-service to their religion. They perform the ritual, but do not carry the spirit behind it into their daily lives. In practice, therefore, the influence of this group is in the direction of rigidity and prejudice, and fails to reflect the ideals of religion.

The philosophers have made as many valuable contributions as the churches to ethics and the art of living, but their most powerful ideas are concealed in a mass of technical verbiage that is incomprehensible to the layman. The psychologists have been chiefly concerned with studying the basic processes of the human mind or with the grossly abnormal, and though such studies are indispensable to our knowledge of man and his behavior, they are of academic rather than of practical interest.

It is the family which is the primary source of emotional education, because the child's greatest need is to be loved. The members of his own family are the most powerful influences upon his emotional and spiritual growth, because from the very beginning of his life he strives to behave and feel in a manner that is pleasing to them. The difficulty is that very many parents are themselves emotionally immature. The emotional climate of their homes is one of conflict and anxiety, and their children do not experience the kind of love and understanding that is necessary for their growth. For every parent who is truly loved and respected, there are twenty whose children dislike, fear or hate them, and are impatient to leave the home. Is this not because the parents have been unable to see their children as individuals, to respect them, to understand their true needs? The great problem that faces all parents is not so much how to exercise discipline and control over their children, but rather how to respect them and guide them towards emotional as well as economic independence. We must learn how to let our children go, and must begin in small ways while they are still very young. All too many parents are unable to release their emotional hold on their children, and many, indeed, fail even to recognize that such a problem exists.

Communication of feeling, too, is vital. If we cannot see a human situation realistically, and express our true feelings about it, we can never teach our children to do so. This lack of communication creates problems in our lives where no problem need have arisen; it holds us back from attaining our dreams; it even prevents us from seeing the richness and beauty that life holds in store for us.

From the time he started his practice as a psychotherapist, List was impressed by the urgency with which the people who came to consult him wanted immediate answers. They did not desire long philosophical abstractions, but simple words and simple answers which they could understand, and could apply immediately to the conduct of their lives. They did not want to stop living while they took four or five years for a full psychoanalysis; they wanted to learn and live at the same time. When they came to List, they found a man overflowing with zest for life, full of warmth and strength and affection for his fellow humans, who believes that though a certain amount of unhappiness is normal (for nobody can escape sickness and disappointments and bereavement), too many of us dissipate our strength being unhappy over situations which we could have avoided if we had learned to channel our energies. While giving full acknowledgment to the greatness of Freud's discoveries, his love of people had always stirred him to rebellion against the disinvolved role of the classical psychoanalyst. He leaned far more towards the views of Sandor

The Man Behind the Method

Ferenczi, who insisted that the healthy love of the therapist for his patient was by far the most active therapeutic agent in any form of counseling or psychotherapy, and that all the theories and techniques should serve only as tools to aid the therapist in reaching his patient, communicating his love, and eliciting a free and healthy response.

Therefore List discarded the traditional couch. He wanted his clients to meet him face to face, to learn to know him as the man he is, rather than as a clinical authority without any personal interest in their lives, and from whose judgments there could be no appeal. List felt that only by this direct contact could he reach them effectively. Only by allowing them to see his personal life openly could he serve as their frame of reference for mature behavior. He was certain that they needed such a frame of reference, for his clients showed him that they had never learned to give or receive a healthy love based on mutual understanding and respect. We are not born with these qualities, nor can we learn them from books. We learn them by imitation, and by making mistakes. We cannot even understand their meaning, unless we have first had the experience of being understood and respected. To achieve this healthy love requires a self-discipline which List tries to instil into every person with whom he works.

In order to learn anything at all we must be able to trust the person who is teaching us, and we must be able to communicate with him. This is where parents so often fail their children. In too many families the expression of feelings is discouraged, and this lack of communication severely hampers the child's emotional growth. If we do not learn how to communicate feelings as a child, it is all the harder to do so as an adult because so much else has to be unlearned. List, therefore, makes extensive use both of group psychotherapy and of more informal group situations, in order to create an emotional climate that fosters freedom of communication, and thus accelerates the learning process.

List has always insisted that the orthodox process of revelation followed by integration is too slow. There is no time to lose in waiting for revelation of the causes underlying the problems, for the person is unhappy and in trouble *now*. Therefore, List immediately looks for his client's strong and healthy areas, and begins integrating him into a new way of life that will make full use of those strengths. As he observes the person's behavior during this process, the sick areas will inevitably reveal themselves, and can be dealt with as they appear. Just as his therapist provides his frame of reference for a mature friendship, so the various groups in the therapeutic community provide the client with an example of healthy family relationship. It is usually assumed that a therapist cannot enter his client's circle of friends, nor take them into his own, without destroying the therapeutic relation. Jacob and Helen List, however, have proved not only that it *is* possible to do so, but also that such a procedure brings excellent results. Because of this close relationship the clients have before them an example of a good marriage. Jacob's clients are also Helen's friends, and her relationship to them is completely independent of their relationship to her husband. For the women, especially, she provides yet another frame of reference—that of the mature woman.

List radiates open friendliness, warmth and strength. He strongly believes that every human being is a combination of talents and character traits which enable him to make a unique and valuable contribution to the society in which he lives. List's own deep sympathy and understanding of human behavior reveal to him the qualities that lie hidden in other people, and his greatest happiness is to see them blossom and come to fruition. He fights fiercely in defense of the values that keep his individuality alive, and will fight *with* as well as *for* his clients, so that they shall learn to recognize their talents and utilize them to the full.

Sophistry and rationalizations do not deceive List; he penetrates directly to the feeling that is implicit in each word, each response. He questions constantly his own motivations, reactions, and attitudes, as he does those of others. He takes nothing for granted. His mind is always open to learn from the most immature as well as from the masters of philosophy. His knowledge of people, of their moods, motivations and emotional needs, has developed his insight to a degree that many people find very disconcerting. His love of people, his belief in God, his conviction that in each of us there is a reflection of

7

God (however dim), have given him a compassion, a strength, and a security that are truly remarkable.

Emerson once remarked that "an institution is the lengthened shadow of one man." This is particularly true of the therapeutic community that has grown up and around him in the years since List first began to practise his method. Almost every conceivable talent and human quality is to be found in it, and in the interaction of the members of the group can be found almost every basic human emotion and situation. There is a sense of unity among the members, and a zest for living. The method teaches them how to live one day at a time, to the full, because the man has discovered in his personal life that this is the best way of living at peace with oneself. He has a sense of fun, an ability to laugh at himself and with others. The joy of living permeates his method, and is radiated by his pupils, who are dearly beloved by him. The method implies a belief in God, or a desire to believe, for without this List's values are negated. It is a therapy based upon education, and reflects his own values, his own security, his own happiness. Many have come prepared to scoff at this method, but have remained to serve. We have found that we share in his happiness and security to the extent that we have accepted his values, and have used them to guide our lives.

CHRISTOPHER TERRY
ALICE REED
New York, 1960

Acknowledgments

I wish to express to my colleagues and students at the Institute of Applied Psychology, Inc., my deep appreciation of the energetic and untiring help they have given me in the rather tiresome tasks of typing and proofreading.

Introduction

A PHILOSOPHY OF PSYCHOTHERAPY

Critics have often accused psychology of being something less than scientific. This accusation has served as a challenge to many in the field who have devoted earnest and untiring effort toward describing human behavior and explaining it in basic and generally applicable terms. The description of phenomena, particularly in terms of cause and effect, is the scientist's main function. He inquires into what *is* and what makes it so.

However, problems of purpose arise when the scientist's findings are applied and utilized. The acquisition of knowledge should never be an end in itself, but the use to which this knowledge will be put is rarely apparent in the material itself. At the point where the descriptions of what *is* give rise to the question of what *should* or *ought* to be, science must give way to philosophy. It is for philosophy, in the light of whatever "truth" science has discovered, to prescribe the "oughts" and "shoulds" necessary to the good life. These philosophical prescriptions determine how best to apply the scientific descriptions to the service of mankind. The current world-wide concern over what best to do with the findings of the nuclear physicists is a most dramatic example of the necessity for science and philosophy to strike a constructive accord.

Psychotherapy, as a method of treatment, is based upon the scientific findings of psychology; therefore, if we conceive of psychotherapy as the application of these scientific principles, we are assuming that its power is *only* to describe and to predict. If, however, the practice of psychotherapy includes the teaching of values and of some kind of prescriptions for a good life, then we have moved into the province of philosophy. As soon as a psychotherapist, either directly or indirectly, indicates the "shoulds" and "oughts," the "goods" and "bads" to a client, he is making a judgment. Furthermore, it is inevitable that every psychotherapist *will* make value judgments. Such common words as normal, abnormal, mature and immature, to say nothing of such diagnostic terms as neurosis, regression and the like, all contain inherent judgments *in the guise of descriptions*. In order to justify the use of value words in any psychotherapeutic method, the practitioner should have a philosophic orientation. Philosophy demands a critical evaluation of the alternatives in any given situation; if we do not evaluate, *we are merely taking the descriptions of psychology and*

A Philosophy of Psychotherapy

using them as prescriptions.

The dichotomy between science and philosophy which has been outlined is not intended to imply a total separation of the two. The same minds which describe can, and often do, prescribe. In the study of human behavior it is imperative that we consider the "oughts" and "shoulds" necessary to the good life. If the knowledge gained from that study is not directed towards the betterment of human life, it either remains useless or, what is worse, becomes a destructive force. Every worker in the field should be ethically and morally dedicated to tie his scientific understanding to a healthy system of "oughts" and "shoulds." Too often, however, this tie is left to chance, and indeed, the influence of the therapist's philosophy and values upon the life of his client is even considered an undesirable variable, to be minimized. It is a fact, I believe, that this variable cannot be eradicated. Nor do I believe that it should be. It is undesirable *only* when it is left unexamined and functions as an unwitting and unconscious part of the relationship between the therapist and his client.

There are good reasons why these ethical and moral principles are so vitally important to the practice of psychotherapy. Here the practitioner accepts the responsibility of profoundly affecting the life of another individual, for when he entitles himself "therapist" he purports to practice a curative or healing art. It has been said that therapy is a form of guidance which merely helps the client to seek and find whatever is for *him* the good life. But no matter how detached and scientifically objective the therapist may be, the close and enduring nature of the therapist-client relationship makes it inevitable that his *own* conception of a good life will, at some level of communication, impinge on the situation. If the therapist can accept this, he can function comfortably in his role knowing that he has examined the "oughts" and "shoulds" of human behavior and is secure in the system or code or way of life to which he subscribes. Whatever his philosophy prescribes as a good life will undoubtedly influence the goals of the therapy he practices.

To my way of thinking, the field which is next-of-kin to psychotherapy is education. In fact I believe them to be so closely interrelated that good psychotherapy is, in great part, education; and good education is, to a large extent, therapeutic. The field of education has produced many philosophers who have dealt prolifically and productively with the problems of methods and goals. That there is much amiss with education is an unfortunate truism; that it is, however, under scrutiny and examination is reassuring and comforting. Educators have always stressed the important role of philosophy, and demand some study of it in the preparation of a teacher. It is unfortunate that the same cannot always be said of those who train psychotherapists.

I am aware that there have been attempts by some psychologists, psychotherapists and particularly psychoanalysts to relate psychology to certain existing systems of philosophy. Some of these attempts have been brilliant contributions for which we should indeed be grateful.

It would be naive and incorrect, however, to assume that there is any single or universal prescription for the good life which might apply and be justified in all situations. Even a perfunctory glance at the history of philosophy confirms this statement. The great minds of all the ages have devised many systems, diverging from each other and splitting hairs in their search for "truth." The diversity of religious beliefs also testifies that no single all-satisfying answer is to be found. Each person has to find what "truth" is for himself, and the values and concepts that he chooses become his personal philosophy.

One thing is very apparent to me; a philosophy must be more than a poetic, high-sounding abstraction. It is worth something only if it works, and it works only if it helps the individuals live. A prescription of "oughts" and "shoulds" must therefore take into account the social and cultural context. The individual who attempts to follow a way of life which is totally out of step with his environment, will hardly be able to realize satisfactions and fulfillment. Much of his time and energy will necessarily go into rebellion, self-justification and deception. A prescription for a good life is valuable only if it is workable when and where it is to be lived. It is useless to prescribe from an idealistic point of view or for a Utopian situation. Let me go on record as saying, however, that I most certainly do not believe that the individual should be adjusted to his environment. There are many forces in society which are unhealthy (here again a judgment

15

must be made). When the social forces are destructive and tend to warp the individual he must be taught to respect his own worth and to preserve himself against those forces.

The modern psychotherapist faces a multitude of problems which are almost overwhelming in their complexity. In our own society with its many subcultures and other groupings, tensions run high and pressures impinge from every quarter. Symptoms of unhappiness and dissatisfaction are rampant; every year more people seek the benefits of psychotherapy. They are unsuccessful in love relationships, or as parents, or as breadwinners, or as students. They are jittery or they are apathetic. They are sleepless or they oversleep. They have no appetite or they are compelled to gluttony. The description of the symptoms is as varied as the number of individuals who describe them. How does the psychotherapist determine the goals of psychotherapy? Obviously one goal which becomes immediately operative is the relief of the described symptoms. But at the point where we begin to consider the basic causes of the symptoms, we must formulate greater and more basic goals. Since psychological problems in our society have attained an incidence which is practically epidemic, it seems probable that they are not unrelated and that there are some basic similarities among them no matter how diverse and unique the individual symptoms. The therapist often faces the question of when to generalize about human behavior and when to be specific. My experience tells me that the human personality is a very specific thing; each is unique and that very fact makes each precious in and of itself. My prime generalization is: let it be so! After that we need employ only those generalizations necessary for the communication which will bring such discrete and diverse entities into harmony.

Fortunately the scientific studies of psychology and the other social sciences have helped to explain some of the phenomena in which many human problems are rooted. Years of empirical observation (the crowd of unhappy faces that have sat before me) seem to indicate that our social structure has produced a lost and lonely breed of man. The struggle for self-realization is thwarted by a society of mass-production, conformity and competition, and particularly the inconsistency between the expressed standards of behavior and the behavior which prevails. I cannot protest too strongly that this inconsistency is a sin against our young people. We are a nation of hypocrites, and by our hypocrisy we are destroying the elements of trust and faith in our youngsters. I have heard it said so many times in so many different ways: "My parents told me about right and wrong. My church told me about right and wrong. My school told me about right and wrong. But everything that I was told is very different from what I have discovered really happens." But the things that were told and repeated so often have a way of clinging, of festering into guilts, of destroying trust in anyone or anything. To me this is the sorriest of tragedies, for faith in the self must be preceded by

17

faith in something outside the self.

From this dim view of society the psychotherapist, as a social critic, can derive one basic goal for the therapeutic process. He must strive to provide a stable frame of reference by which his client can consistently evaluate himself and others. This enables the client to develop a personal system of "oughts" and "shoulds," which will permit him to achieve a good life for himself and a respect for the rights of others. I believe that this function as a frame of reference is no mere accident or by-product of the treatment process; but is a fundamental requirement if the method is to help the client assemble an integrated and mature personality from his kaleidoscopic emotional chaos. He was originally socialized into confusion. He must now be re-socialized into maturity. He must be cast in healthier roles and exposed to healthier norms. Here again the responsibility for value judgments (the choice of those roles and norms) rests with the therapist.

Self-understanding or the achievement of a realistic self-image is frequently mentioned as a goal of psychotherapy. To direct the therapeutic process toward this static and isolated end, however, would be impossible and foolish. The self is a dynamic entity in constant interaction with its environment. The therapy is certainly healing or curative to whatever degree it succeeds in helping the individual client toward becoming a realistically defined person in *constructive* interaction with his environment. All very well and good—but what's the rental on an ivory tower these days? Let's not forget for one moment that the environment had everything to do with the distortion of the self-image which burdens the client when he comes into therapy. And the environment, in general, is not going to change very much. The new ingredient included in the client's environment at this point is the therapist. Any new interaction, any healthier interaction starts then and there. It is a crucial time, a time for hope and a time for courage. But the relationship will only take root, the hope and the courage will only emerge if the therapist cares—not cares to build his reputation, not cares to earn a fee, but genuinely feels the worthiness of the person with whom he is working and willingly demonstrates that feeling by investing a part of himself in the relationship. That investment, I believe, is a commitment to the client, a commitment to fight for him and with him, a commitment to a sharing and an honesty which allows the therapist no refuge on a pedestal.

Life has taught me that freedom is very precious—and usually very hard to come by. It must be earned and must constantly be protected. Free will in the matter of choice and decisions is largely determined by early learning and conditioning. For that reason a healthier concept of both the self and the environment is the only instrument by which an individual can gain any modicum of personal freedom and accept his mature responsibilities to himself and to society. Personal freedom is synonymous with the psychological term "personal security." If the environment is perceived as threatening there can be no freedom, no security. Because I place so high a value on freedom, and because I dare to judge the environment which curtails it, I dare to manipulate the environment of the client in order to provide constructive situations. We cannot wait for evolution, or even revelation. The present is the only time we ever really have. Can we wait until tomorrow to live? Tomorrow does not exist. And having problems is no reason to postpone living. In fact, wherever possible I say, "Postpone the problems and make *today* pay off with something constructive." I have many times seen problems postponed so long in the interest of other activities that somehow they were lost along the way. To me that is freedom in action. Involvement in enriching experiences at the expense of old fears or guilts or angers is trading chains for wings.

Freedom, or call it by its other name, security, is learned, and it begins to be learned in that initial commitment which takes place in the therapist's office. You cannot learn freedom in a cage or constantly facing a boundary. The therapist can do a great deal to remove the bars and the boundaries when he meets the client honestly and directly. But let me stress again that caring for the client as an individual must be a genuine feeling. Trust cannot be engendered and the feeling of threat dispelled in a situation which is simulated or counterfeit. However, the communication of the warmth of a genuine caring will foster the first timid flights of freedom more surely than will anything else.

A Philosophy of Psychotherapy

If the freedom, or security, that we have been talking about is one of the goals of therapy, then we must consider another which is inseparable from it. Freedom carries a price tag, that is, it goes hand in hand with responsibility. To be free is to be strong, but strength can be destructive as well as constructive. If one exercises his freedom at someone else's expense, he is not free as we have used the word; he is more likely an irresponsible bully whose motivation is unhealthy. This sense of responsibility which must be developed is called maturity. Emotional maturity is not an easy concept to grasp because it is an ongoing process. Every new level of development in the personality which defines and strengthens the self-image encourages the individual to expect more and more of himself and to become less and less dependent upon others. The relatively mature person who chooses not to conform to some standard or expectation does so, not out of sheer rebellion, but with full awareness of any consequences involved and the willingness to accept them. I maintain that clients must first learn this sense of responsibility through the application of external discipline. The freedoms enjoyed in my office (and they are many, as the other chapters of this volume indicate) carry with them certain responsibilities; privileges, on the other hand, must be earned. Although this has been an over-simplification of the concept of maturity, I believe, nevertheless, that its two major ingredients are self-respect and independence.

After my ardent plea that philosophy be set as a watchdog over scientific psychology as applied in psychotherapy, I may well be asked: "But just what is your philosophy?" I answer: "It has no name." If any philosophical label can be pinned on me at all, I suppose it could be that of "eclectic." I have studied the famous philosophers, and they have all made their mark on my thinking. My religion, too, no doubt, made its contribution. I continue to read contemporary philosophical writers, and always find new and stimulating views of the age-old problems. Therefore, I can claim little that is original except for the fact that these many views of God and of man, of purpose and of values, have been singularly amalgamated within the context of my own life experience. How much the ideas were tempered by the experience, and the experience by the ideas, can never be known. The result, however, is that I respect a loving, understanding and forgiving God who sees in what I give to my fellow creatures my gift to Him. I believe that man is fundamentally good, and it is the basis of my work that I try to help free him to be good. I believe the purpose of life is service and that nothing gives meaning to life so much as the fulfillment of work well done, and then shared. To be fulfilled through good work is to love oneself, and to share selflessly is to love others. I believe that each day is an opportunity to experience these things and to come a little closer to their finer accomplishment. All this I *believe*. What I *know* is that life can be very difficult and that the pitfalls and barriers along the way are many. I have marked some of them as I have come along. If I can spare waste and frustration in the lives of others by sharing this knowledge, I shall be satisfied with my purpose. My methods are not perfect. They will not work miracles for everyone, but some of those who have been willing to learn have been helped to work their own miracles.

Chapter I

THE THERAPEUTIC COMMUNITY

The List Method of Psychotherapy is not emergency treatment for spiritual casualties, but rather teaches a whole way of life. The philosophy behind the method is a philosophy of education—education for living. Those who practice this method are therefore educators, not psychologists. Instead of placing our clients on a couch and analyzing their childhood, we teach them how to live right now. For the people we work with, the past is a canceled check. We deal with their problems of living right here in the present, with the expectation that what they learn from their experiences, under our guidance, will make their future happier and more successful.

There are very many people who have not learned the art of living, and are therefore dissatisfied with their lives. This art is not an academic subject taught in our schools and universities, and it is unfortunately one which few parents have mastered. A child, therefore, often matures physically without growing up emotionally. He receives instruction in reading and writing, music and dance, arithmetic and history, but the most important part of his education is neglected. He is not shown how to evaluate situations; how to recognize and handle his emotions; how to distinguish between his dream world and the reality; how to observe and understand other people. He is not taught to recognize and utilize the strengths and weaknesses of his own character. If he has any sense of his own identity, of his own worth, it is because he has acquired it by painful gropings through the maze of customs and mores in which he has been brought up. And so, although he may be able to play the violin, solve differential equations, and pour tea, he has not acquired the basic tools that he needs in order to be master of himself. It is when he discovers that he is not his own master nor living the kind of life he would like to lead, that he reaches out for help. The List Method aims to teach such people an emotionally, intellectually and spiritually balanced way of living. To learn a whole new way of life is by no means easy for an adult. There is much to be unlearned as well as to be learned, and the prospect of such radical changes can be quite overwhelming. A beginning must be made somewhere, however, and since small changes are easier to make than large far-reaching ones, the List Method concentrates upon simplifying life, living one day at a time, and taking one thing at a time.

I do not mean that no thought should be given to the

future. On the contrary, it is very necessary to keep constantly in mind the goals that one wishes to achieve. But today these goals are only a dream, and many days or even years must pass before they can become a reality. Each choice that we make today determines the choices that are open to us tomorrow, and so it is vital to be sure that today's time is not wasted. We have to make the decisions that seem to lead us most surely in the direction of our goal, bearing in mind that each choice must be based on reality, on the talents and information that we have at hand. When you drive from New York to Buffalo it is first necessary to know how to get out of New York onto a highway that leads towards Buffalo. You cannot be certain that you will be able to keep to that road; a storm may block it and force you into a detour. Still less do you need to consult the street map with all the details of Buffalo until you are on the outskirts of the town. I know one lady who is planning to sell her house and buy an apartment in a project whose foundations have only just been laid. Yet when I talked with her about it, she had already started planning the color scheme of the kitchen and what she was going to say to the grocer who would surely fail to deliver her groceries on the first day she occupied the apartment. These are details that today are still in the realm of fantasy. The details that belong in today's reality are making an appointment with her lawyer to discuss putting down a deposit on the apartment, and other such items. Unless these are accomplished now, her color scheme will be wasted, and it will be some other person's order that the grocer defaults on. Do today what belongs to today, so that tomorrow there will be something on which to build.

That is what I mean "living one day at a time." Whenever you are confronted with a task which seems overwhelming, break it down into smaller parts. Some of these parts may be difficult for you, but the energy that you save by not worrying about how you are going to get the whole job done can be profitably applied to completing the sections one by one to the very best of your ability. Doing one thing at a time simplifies life tremendously. Living one day at a time, taking one thing at a time, means learning to compartmentalize one's life, and to keep emotions that go with one situation from spilling over where they do not belong. It means bending all one's energies to the immediate task, and making the most of what is at hand. If a business man allows himself to be distracted from his work by thoughts and angers which belong with his wife, he may antagonize an important client. If he allows the frustrations of his work to affect his behavior towards his wife, he risks damaging his relationship to her. Of course he may talk to her about his difficulties, but he must never lose sight of the fact that she is not personally involved in them, and he must be able to put aside the anger that he has felt at work in order to be able to give his wife a loving greeting when his day's work is over.

There is a prayer which says: "God grant me the strength to accept those things which cannot be changed;

the courage to change those things which can be changed; and the wisdom to know the difference between the two." For the person who lives one day at a time, life is a relatively simple matter, and its simplicity makes it enjoyable. He wakes up each morning thanking God that he is alive. He does not concern himself with the details of tomorrow, for he cannot know if God will grant him another day.

The person who follows this philosophy finds that his problems slip into their proper perspective, so that he is able to handle things as they occur. If one is not sure that tomorrow will come, he must do those tasks which are immediately at hand, without procrastinating. His work is done punctually, and he has leisure in which to play.

My clients do not at first find this philosophy an easy one to follow. They have been too used to living in the past, present and future all at the same time, and they have taken this confusion as a part of the normal course of life. Sometimes I say to them, "If you knew for sure that today was your last day on earth, what would you do with it?" Usually this brings them up short, and makes them take a good look at the way they are living. After they have told me the things they would like to do, I say to them, "How do you know that it isn't your last day?" This causes further confusion, until they become accostumed to the idea that when they go to bed at night, they don't know for sure whether they will wake up the next morning. How simple everything becomes when one lives by this premise! How ordered one's life can be if he practices it!

We then begin to get down to specifics in our conversation. I say to them, "When you wake up in the morning you have two choices for your day—you can be happy or unhappy. It is as simple as that. You are the one who decides how your day shall run. You cannot place the decision with anyone else. It is up to you—do you want to have a happy day or an unhappy one?" The response is always yes, they want a happy day. Then I say to them, "Since you have made the choice, expect the best, for if you expect the best you will get it. If you expect the worst, that will happen also. You must meet life head-on and give it every bit of yourself. Hold nothing back from life. Now that you only have one day in which to live, where do you want to go? What do you want out of life?" We then discuss the things that he has always wanted to do, and go about setting up a program that will enable him to live his twenty-four hours happily and contentedly.

A firm belief in God is the most important power in an individual's life. The ritual by which he worships God is unimportant; the recognition that there *is* a God, is vital. No person is mature unless he recognizes that there is a power greater than himself. We must also give recognition to the divine spark within us which enables us to grow, to turn away from the state of childhood in which our responses to a situation are imposed on us from without; it moves us towards a state of maturity in which we know our strengths and weaknesses, and are so in control of them that we can take responsibility for our actions. The recognition that we have the capacity to do this, and that as unique individuals we each have a role to play in life, is the state of grace without which we cannot know the joys of life. One of the first questions which I ask of a new client is, "Do you believe in God?" If the answer is "No, and I do not wish to learn," then I cannot work with this person, for such a response implies a deep rejection of all my values, of man's capacity for growth, and indeed of life itself.

Clients usually come to us for help in learning how to live, either because they have never had any faith in themselves, or because they have lost whatever faith they once had. Often they do not have faith in anyone or anything. Sometimes they need something that they can actually hold, in order to take the first steps in developing faith in themselves and in others. When this is the case I often give them a small mustard seed enclosed in a plastic bubble and tell them how Jesus once said to his disciples: "If ye have faith as a grain of mustard seed, ye shall say unto this mountain, 'Remove hence to yonder place,' and it shall remove; and nothing shall be impossible unto you." (Matthew 17:19.) Many clients have told me of their experiences with this small reminder of faith. Frequently the story goes something like this: "I was afraid of the exam, Dr. List. I felt I would fail my course. But then I put my hand in my pocket and felt the mustard seed, and I remembered what you said. I remembered that you had faith that I could pass the exam and so I sat down and tried very hard to answer the questions." With the mustard seed as a physical reminder that someone believes in them, the clients take their first steps toward a faith in their own abilities.

But living involves relations with other people, as well as a belief in God. Most of the clients who come in have not been successful in their interpersonal relationships, because they have never learned how to relate to people. When we discuss their relationships I sometimes tell them a story to show that people need one another; that although the client may not be able to take care of all his needs, he can be taught to fill others' needs, and so in turn his own will be met.

A man once asked to be shown the difference between Heaven and Hell, and was taken into the lower regions to see a large banquet hall, beautifully decorated, whose tables were loaded with delicious foods. The luxury and comfort at first amazed him. But on looking closely at the diners he saw that they were thin and miserable because their hands were chained together and they could not bring their forks to their mouths. There was an abundance of food in front of their eyes yet they were starving. Upon reaching Heaven he found a banquet hall identical to the one in Hell. Here, too, the diners were chained together, but they were smiling, and appeared healthy and happy. As he looked at them he understood the difference between the two places. Since the heavenly people could not reach their own mouths, each man loaded his fork with food from his own plate, and reached over to the person sitting next to him. Each man was feeding his neighbor.

It is we ourselves who make a heaven or a hell of our life on earth. Those who isolate themselves are truly miserable creatures, starving to death with food in front of them. We teach our people that man cannot live in isolation, and that he must do for others and allow others to do for him. When he learns this he forms deeper, more loving and more trusting relationships with those around him. His own life is broadened and enriched, and as he brings happiness to others so he brings more happiness to himself.

The client learns how to be a friend; how to ask, and how to give. He is shown that he and his friend can be together and yet retain separate identities; he learns to give his best to his friend, but also to allow him his peace and privacy; to hold close with open hands.

The client is taught how to give, by learning first to examine himself to see if he is worthy to be a giver. He is taught how to receive, without feeling the debt of the receiver, which denies the gift.

He is taught how to ask for the things which he truly needs, and how to accept them with love and graciousness. He learns that only when he gives of himself does he truly give.

He learns that there are times in his life when he must depend upon others, and times when he must depend wholly upon himself. The mature individual recognizes these times and acts accordingly.

We show our clients that nothing is really worth doing

unless it is done with enjoyment and with love. Without love everything becomes empty and worthless. It is when he does his work with love that he forges a link from himself to others and to God.

Each client who desires to learn to live a day at a time also implies that he wants to learn how to belong to himself. He must learn to trust his feelings as a guide to his conduct. However, he cannot do this unless he learns to recognize his strengths and weaknesses, and to accept them with the knowledge that he can change them if he so desires. Sometimes the client feels that to do this he must hitch his wagon to a star, and he is perfectly right. How can we go on living unless we have a dream and follow it to completion? Emerson wrote: "Sin is when a man is untrue to his own constitution." If human beings do not have the courage to follow the law of their own bodies then they will never know real contentment or joy, or be able to give them to others.

We can do anything which we believe we can. It is only fear which holds us back from our goals, and fear can be conquered. Sometimes on the road to the fulfillment of his dream the client will stumble and fall. But what does this matter? All that can happen is that he will get himself covered with a little dirt, or collect a few scars. Once he picks himself up and again stands firmly upon his own two feet, he will be less afraid of another tumble. Emerson advised: "Try the rough water as well as the smooth. Rough water can teach lessons worth knowing."

It is much easier to write about living one day at a time

than to put the idea into practice in one's life. The specific ways in which we teach our clients how to do so will be described in later chapters, but if these are to be understood, it is important to have as clear a picture as possible of the setting in which our teaching takes place.

Psychoanalytic practice regards the analytic period in a sense as "time out" from living, and discourages the patient under analysis from making any decisions which will markedly affect the course of his life. The first phase of the analysis reveals the patient's defense mechanisms and distortions, mainly through exploration of his childhood experiences. Only towards the end of the analysis can he attempt to integrate his new knowledge about himself into his life. The people I work with are able to function almost normally in many areas, and I believe that it is a waste of time to make exploration of their childhood the chief therapeutic technique. When he comes to me, the client has certain characteristic ways of behaving, which prevent him from forming satisfactory personal relationships and making full use of his talents. While he remains in the same environment it is impossible for him either to identify or to change these behavior patterns, which are necessary for his survival there. My aim is to give him a new way of life altogether, and to start integrating him at once into a different and more favorable environment. It is during the process of integration that he begins to identify his patterns, and to understand the conditions which made them necessary to him.

Education for Living

Psychoanalysis would have the patient stand still in life. I want my client to move forward, to meet new experiences both inside and outside the therapeutic setting. If he is to do so with trust and confidence, he must be provided with an environment that is favorable to change and to the free communication of feelings, and that will permit him to develop satisfying personal relationships. The new environment must be powerful enough to offset the retarding influences of his home environment, particularly when he must exist in both at the same time. Since the client's unhealthy patterns are basically reactions either to a deprivation of healthy love, or to parental rejection of his own expressions of love, the new environment must above all be accepting, and be characterized by an atmosphere of warmth and affection.

The prototype of this environment developed in my own reception room. In orthodox settings the client comes into the office only to keep his appointments. My first clients, like many of those who come to me today, felt very much alone in their struggle. They had acquaintances, but no friends. Because they were lonely, I suggested that they come to my office at times other than their scheduled appointments. They began to sit and talk in my reception room, and found that there was much that they could learn from each other. When several were present, and I had free time, we would talk informally about every aspect of life. As they grew to know and understand each other, my reception room became their regular meeting place after work and school. Our discussion groups became more frequent, and began to probe more deeply into the relationships between them. These close contacts between my clients provided much material for discussion both in private sessions and in the group. Their vigorous efforts towards honesty and mutual respect greatly accelerated their growth, and it might be said that the therapeutic setting extended outward from my office to any place in the city where two or more of my clients were spending time together.

This first group of clients formed the nucleus of the therapeutic community which exists today. Several of them proved to be so rich in the human qualities required by a therapist, that after gaining the requisite academic qualifications they became my colleagues, and have built up successful practices of their own. They encourage their clients to get to know me, and to make friends among the people who frequent our joint reception room. Thus, the total therapeutic community is made up of many constellations, and its members are united by links of many different kinds. The closest friendships are often, though not always, formed between clients who work with the same therapist and attend the same formal therapeutic group. But they all have direct access to me, and this gives them a common bond which unifies the entire therapeutic setting, and makes of it one large family.

The clients' encounters in the large and small acts of daily living, although superficially resembling similar contacts with people in the larger world, are in fact different in one very important respect. They occur under the observation and protection of the therapists, between people who share the desire to know and understand themselves and others.

The number and diversity of the personalities encompassed within the therapeutic community makes of it a microcosmos where, sooner or later, there occurs almost every basic human situation that could occur in the larger world. Not only are the client's loves, anxieties, fears, angers, jealousies, successes and failures in outside situations brought into the community for analysis and re-evaluation, but similar events also arise in the community, where the client is not allowed to ignore, distort, or forget them. The analysis of these incidents, while they are still fresh in the minds of the participants, becomes a source of great strength that can be carried into other situations.

Every event of daily living that takes place within the community can be used therapeutically. It is, of course, impossible for each client to have a good relationship with all of the others; but whether people like or dislike each other, they are sooner or later forced into at least superficial contact in the reception room. In ordinary society, one can avoid people one dislikes, or disparage them, or politely demolish them, without having to think much about one's own motives. Here one is drawn to some people, and repelled by others; but one's behavior is under observation. It is not enough, in the therapeutic community, to say "I don't like Jane!" If the client is truly interested in understanding himself and others it is important for him to explore the reasons why he does not like Jane. Perhaps it is because she is fat, and he does not like obesity. Perhaps she resembles his sister, whom he cannot tolerate. Perhaps it is because she has a withered arm and he fears deformities. Whatever the reason, he must explore it if he truly desires to learn about himself. In outside situations the individual seldom examines himself to this extent, because he is conditioned to say "I don't like so-and-so" and let it go at that. The other party also is willing to let the contact die and so both people lose what might have been a fine friendship, or at least the opportunity to develop respect for each other.

It must be realized that, granting our people eight hours of sleep each night, they still have 110 waking hours of the week in which to get into trouble. On the average, each client has only one hour with his therapist in which to repair the damage to himself and others, and one hour of group session for further exploration of his behavior and feelings. This is why the therapeutic community is so valuable to him. Time spent with any of its members is well spent, because it inevitably leads to the production of incidents and material which accelerate his progress in therapy. Casual meetings, big parties, expeditions to the beach or theatre, all help to reveal his behavior patterns. Each and every situation can be turned into a learning process for one who truly desires to move forward in self-understanding. The therapeutic community as a whole, has the role of observer and mirror. Here the client's self concept and behavior is reflected in other people's reactions to him. Through others he is able to determine the kind of a person he is at the time, and with them he grows toward maturity.

The therapeutic community also plays a supportive role. The moment a new member enters the community, he immediately has two firm supports in all aspects of life, even though he may not realize it at the time. The first is his therapist, with whom he gradually establishes a relationship which is on a much deeper level than any he has ever had before in his life. The second is the person who recommended him to his therapist.* This friend becomes his own special support, who introduces him to other people, shows him around the premises, and works closely with the therapist, watching over him to give him whatever information and moral or physical support he may need. If the new member starts upon a program of higher education, for example, his friend will go with him to help him register in college. At the earliest possible moment, the new arrival will be introduced into a therapeutic group, and it is here, where he finds freedom and acceptance to a degree that he has probably never before experienced, that he also finds constant support.

---

* I would like to make it clear, at this point, how our clients come to us. Because all the clients are so closely bound together in a therapeutic community whose relationships are those that one would expect to find in a healthy family atmosphere, I must exercise every precaution for their protection. My colleagues and I have therefore made it a rule never to accept any person who is not personally known to, and recommended by, at least one of our own clients.

The Therapeutic Community

As he becomes secure in the group, he finds that there are people who are genuinely concerned about him, who want to like him, who are happy with his successes. Even if they do not like his behavior, they recognize his worth as a person struggling toward life. For this reason alone (if for no other), they are always willing to help him through the tasks he finds difficult, not because he has done anything for them as yet, but because he is now a member of the group which in the past helped them in the same way. There is a feeling of solidarity; each person contributes his talents, and by giving freely to others brings those talents alive. If the new member decides to leave home and live on his own for the first time, members of the group will help him to find an apartment, or some member will share one with him; the group will help him find furniture and decorate the apartment. If he dreads an appointment concerning a job, someone who is more secure in that area will go with him as far as the outer office, to keep him company and give moral support. If he is involved in an unhappy marriage, he will always find someone who will listen to his troubles when his therapist is not available. In any crisis of life he can call for help of any kind, and know that his call will be answered.

The person who is unhappy, who distrusts himself and has never learned to trust others, cannot at first believe that help of this kind can be given freely. But unless he stubbornly covers his ears and refuses to believe the evidence of his eyes about what happens to other people in such situations he must eventually come to believe it. And if he is wise, and is genuinely trying to find a better way of life than he had before he entered therapy, he will allow himself to become involved in such activities. He may go to twenty parties, and because of his own self-involvement may never get nearer to knowing any of the other people. But let him spend an afternoon with another member of the group, scraping the floors and painting the walls of someone else's apartment, and he can hardly fail to recognize whether his companion is an eager or a lazy workman, cooperative or arrogant, skilled or clumsy, willing to take or delegate responsibility. He will reveal himself to the same degree even if he is not aware of it; if he is perceptive, he will even discover surprising things about himself during the course of the work.

It is at the point where he is beginning to find security in the therapy group, and security in one or two friends with whom he has an even closer relationship, that the support of the group is most valuable to him. By this time he is beginning to find some strength of his own, but it is not yet sufficient to allow him to handle any major upheavals in his life. No one can survive, still less make progress, unless he feels secure that he has a place where he belongs and people who love him. This is where the group comes in. The group is his new family, and with its support he can make the next steps on the road toward his goal.

This new family is entirely different from his old one. The protective screens of sex, occupation and status have been stripped away, and people have to relate directly to other people. In the final analysis it is not possible for anyone to relate to a group as such; the group process is a quick succession of interactions with individual members. Success in relating to a group depends upon one's success in his relationships to individuals and upon one's ability to perceive and maintain a proper perspective between the individual relationships. By making use of the therapeutic community the client learns skillful management of interpersonal relations of all kinds. As always, when learning new skills people make many mistakes at first, but these mistakes do not have the damaging effect on their sense of worth that similar mistakes in the larger world would have. They gradually learn that flexibility is a prerequisite for maturity, that there are many paths to each goal, and that if one path is blocked it is possible to backtrack and find another one, which may be better than the first. As they learn this new way of life in the protected setting of the community, they find that each step, each success, and even each mistake which has been identified and analyzed, gives them greater security in their relationships outside the community. To be sure, it is not possible to call the shots in the larger world in quite the same way as in the therapeutic community, but they can use the awareness and strength they have gained to build better relationships, to smooth their path, and to protect themselves. They function better in the world because they have learned that they have something to give to the world, and have also learned how to give it.

Education for Living

The therapeutic community, as we use it, is in reality a laboratory for living. Just as the biology professor moves his students from the lecture hall into the lab to practice what he has taught them, so we move our clients into the therapeutic community to make practical use of the knowledge they have gained in their therapist's office. The workings of the community are very exciting and rewarding to watch. In one particular week, for example, there was a major unheaval in the lives of three clients, and in each case many of the others at once involved themselves to help. First, one of the women had decided to move from her country home into a city apartment. Although living in the city would be far more convenient for her, to say nothing of the fact that living alone in a large house filled with the ghosts of twenty-five years was harmful to her, she still felt very afraid of this big step. A friend called her one evening and said "Mary, I'm very angry with you. I have offered to help you pack three times, and each time you have put me off. Don't you need any help? Are you angry with me for some reason that I don't know about?" Mary was not angry with her friend. She simply did not know how to ask for help. She feared that her friend did not truly want to help her, but was merely "being nice" and so she had not responded to the offer. Her friend was not so easily put off, however. She got into her car and drove to the country to find Mary in tears, utterly immobilized by the thought of leaving her home, unable even to begin planning the move. Her friend knew exactly how Mary felt because

44

she herself had made a similar move the year before with the help of the group. She set to and helped Mary organize the move from beginning to end, staying with her when the vans came, and helping her to settle in her new apartment.

The same week Grace was suddenly struck with an attack of appendicitis and reached for the phone to call a friend who lived in the neighborhood. Her friend rushed over, called the doctor, and then took her to the hospital. In the meantime other clients had been notified and while one of them called her doctor brother to perform the operation, another came to take Grace's young daughter to her home while she was in the hospital.

Also during this particular week a third client moved his business to a larger office, and many clients were happily helping him to plan the decor, paint, move furniture, and shop.

Isolated events? Unusual events? Not in the least. Similar things happen all the time in life, and in the therapeutic community the clients learn how to give and how to receive, how to love, to be a friend. They give parties for each other, exchange furniture and clothing, help each other to study, give each other emotional support when needed. In short, here, in the laboratory for living they learn all those things which they should have learned to do as children, but for some unfortunate reason did not.

The therapeutic community does not confine itself to this type of activity. Many of the clients have their own special God-given talents. Some are skilled artists, writers, musicians, and they share their knowledge with those who desire it. Several of the members dance extremely well and have organized a dancing class. A ceramist teaches pottery. A music therapist gives music lessons. A writer teaches a class in creative writing. An artist gives lessons. Each of these classes has a specific purpose and each instructor has a goal to fulfill. Each tries to share his own particular talents with others—whatever he gives, he receives in return many-fold. The classes also become a learning experience for the teacher, who is forced to reach his students on an emotional as well as an intellectual level. Their response encourages him to place a proper value on his abilities.

Each client's main problems lie in his relationship to himself; his understanding of himself and the manner in which he accepts or rejects himself. When he is in accord with himself all his problems fade away. It is when he is not in accord with himself that he is at odds with the rest of the world. This is the reason why it is so very important for him to take one step at a time in his daily living. By living a day at a time he learns to live an hour at a time and finally a minute at a time. Since yesterday is already behind him and tomorrow may never come, many pressures are removed from his life and he becomes free. He learns to say to himself "This is true at *this* time" or "This must be handled at *this* time" and as long as he attends to those things which belong to this time only, he becomes able to handle any situation which

46

may arise in his daily living without bringing confusion to his life. By taking care of today, those things which belong to tomorrow (if there will be a tomorrow for him) will then fall into place.

We teach our clients that attitudes are more important than facts. Facts can be handled when they are perceived in the light of good attitudes. It is only when the client applies bad attitudes to facts that he is thrown into confusion and often becomes immobilized.

In living one day at a time the person's attitude toward life is of the utmost importance. If he starts each day with a happy, peaceful, contented expectation that the day will go well, it will go well for him. He should end each day in the same manner, and just before he falls asleep each night, he can relax himself into a peaceful slumber by thanking God for his happy day. It is also good for him to look back over the events of the day and to select the happiest of them to think over before falling asleep. The incident may be a very small one; his son may have said "I love you" in a very special way; or he may have stopped to watch a robin build its nest; or perhaps he may have done some small favor for a friend. Whatever the happiest moment was, if he relives it before he falls asleep he can reaffirm the fact that his attitude is more important than anything else in living.

Many philosophers have spoken about the power which attitudes have over the life of an individual. William James felt that "human beings can alter their lives by altering their attitudes"; Marcus Aurelius said "A man's life is what his thoughts make of it." Emerson wrote, "A man is what he thinks about all day long." By thinking good thoughts; by getting rid of bad attitudes; by living a day at a time; taking each thing step by step, we can lead the kind of lives we desire, and therefore become the kind of human beings we have dreamed about.

In a therapeutic setting where there is no social contact between therapist and client or between the clients themselves, an education of this kind is impossible. I believe that full use of the therapeutic community greatly accelerates our people's education toward maturity. The competent therapist can help his client to discover the strengths of his character and help him to eliminate his weaknesses, but without using the therapeutic community this will be a much longer process. If the client is allowed to enjoy contact with his therapist and with other clients outside of the therapeutic session in actual life situations, his growth toward maturity will be greatly accelerated. In fact, the more he dares to expose himself to situations and to people, the faster he will move in his therapy, provided he is willing and able to look at himself realistically. Much of the material discussed in his private session comes from the client's experiences in living in the therapeutic community.

Love is the most powerful therapeutic agent known; and that love can flower only in a setting where there can be a sense of belonging, and opportunity to get to know and to understand many different types of people. There must be a complete freedom to express both affection and hostility, and indeed every kind of feeling. In the therapeutic community every one of our clients has the opportunity to encounter new people and new ideas, to see the reaction of these people to his own ideas and moods, and to feel the acceptance that he seeks.

The therapeutic community thus becomes for each client a new family—one in which he is accepted for himself as a unique individual of worth. This family shows him the affection they feel toward him, helps him whenever help is needed, and in short becomes his frame of reference for living a life which will be satisfactory and constructive for him. It is not grasping; does not demand of him more than he is capable of giving; shows him the respect that is due to him as a human being; desires for him the best that life can offer. And so this new family sends him back out into the larger world to learn how to deal with a multitude of situations which, because of his experiences in the protective climate of the therapeutic community, he suddenly finds that he can handle in a new, mature manner. He remains in the community by his own choice, not by its demand. He learns to see unique individuals, no longer lost in a crowd which he feels is hostile to him and which he must fight in order to obtain what he desires.

His security that there is a place where he is loved, respected and at home, makes all his learning in the therapeutic community invaluable to him. And what he learns about people and situations in the therapeutic community, he learns to extend into the larger world. He then finds, because of his experiences in this laboratory for living, that he can function in life as he desires—more maturely, with less fear, and at peace within himself.

Chapter II

THE CLIENT-THERAPIST RELATIONSHIP

In all forms of psychotherapy it is the personality of the therapist that holds the key to the success or failure of the therapy. Whether the analyst be a Freudian, a neo-Freudian, a follower of Adler, Jung, Horney or Sullivan, whether he places his patient on a couch or on a chair, is directive or non-directive, it is he who provides the frame of reference from which his client will eventually view himself and the world. The client who seeks him out is a person who is disoriented, unable to trust himself or others, and whose inner picture of himself and his environment differs from the reality. Such a person is driven hither and yon by his desires, or by habit patterns formed long ago. He controls neither his feelings nor his behavior; rather, they control him. But his arrival in the therapist's office signifies that this puppet is seeking to become a free human being, capable of exercising such free choice as the structure of society permits, and of contributing to the growth and maturity of that society within the limits of his potentialities. It follows that the kind of human being he is to *become*, is largely determined by the kind of human being his therapist *is*. By whatever method he works, the therapist is necessarily an educator, a teacher. No teacher, however, can raise his pupil above his own level of intellectual or emotional maturity. For the client, therefore, the quality of the relationship he is able to build with his therapist is of the highest importance to his own growth and development. It becomes the pattern for all subsequent relationships he may develop, because it is in the therapist's thinking and behavior that he finds the new concept of maturity that will replace the inadequate one drawn from his parents. The therapist is doing the job that they left incomplete.

Over the years I have found myself in ever increasing disagreement with the impersonal, disinvolved type of approach to the client-therapist relationship which was common in the 1930's, and is still held by certain schools of thought. This type of relationship results in a dichotomy between client and therapist, whose spheres of activity never meet outside the therapeutic setting. In the List Method there is no dichotomy between therapist and client. The therapist must constantly view himself as a client, more advanced along the road to maturity than those he teaches, but constantly growing and learning. This principle stems from the belief that every individual is entitled to his unique self, and to his personal expression of it. Embracing this principle, however, carries with it the responsibility for developing that self to the fullest of its powers. The mature person has dared to face the truth about himself and his environment, to deal with it realistically, and to integrate it into his total personality; he leads a life in which this process is constantly operating, and is constantly re-examined. The therapist, therefore, provides a frame of reference as to what constitutes mature behavior. In order to be capable of this, he must himself be very secure, constantly open to fresh experiences, and humble enough to be willing to learn from his clients.

Thus, the therapist uses the accumulated experiences and wisdom of his entire life, and whatever he accomplishes with his client he accomplishes only because of who and what he is. In order to help the client understand him as a man, the therapist must constantly and consistently reveal himself. Both will profit from the experience if the therapist shares the events which have occurred in his personal life. The mother who is working through a problem with her son's teacher will feel close to a therapist who says, "When my son was your boy's age we had a similar problem. Let me tell you how we handled it, and we'll see if this would work for you in your situation." Not only will the mother find a solution to her problem during this discussion, but she will also learn about her therapist as a human being.

This is why I have always insisted that the therapist

must not be a remote, disinvolved figure, in whose personal life the client has no part, and who in turn plays no part in the client's life except during their professional contacts. I believe that all of us who work with people in this instructive capacity must truly love them, or the therapy will not be successful. The therapist must first love his client before he can teach the client to love him; he must first accept the client before the client will be able to accept himself. Love, then, is the positive force which enables the client to change his life. The client is taught first how to respect himself, and then how to respect others. It is the therapist's love for his client, given freely and with spontaneity, which provides the climate of trust, confidence and hope which is necessary for the client's emotional growth.

The creation of such a climate makes heavy demands upon both client and therapist. First and foremost, if there is to be any relationship at all, the therapist must be able to discern in his client some quality that he can like, wholeheartedly and without reservations. If he does not like his client there is no chance of the relationship developing to any depth. Sooner or later the client will detect the dislike, through a word, a look, a silence, and from that moment the relationship is doomed. It may linger on for a while, but eventually he will terminate the treatment and leave. "Liking" a person has nothing to do with his behavior. It is a quality that the therapist is looking for, not an act. The person may be mean to his wife and children, horrible to his employees, rude and hostile to the therapist, but this is on the surface. If he responds in any way, by a look, an expression, a word, that gives some indication that there is hidden away in a corner of his heart one warm feeling for somebody other than himself, one generous impulse that is seeking an outlet, this is something that the therapist can like, and can build upon.

Therefore, right from the first meeting, providing that I can find some quality in the client that I can like and respect, and can call up some response from him, however feeble, to my own personality, I can begin to establish my relationship with the client by saying to him "I *like* you, and I want to help you to like yourself." Remember, in saying this I am making no statement about his past, present or future behavior. I am saying that whatever impression he may have of himself, here at last is one person who can wholeheartedly say "I *like* you. Let's go."

This is the vital moment upon which the success of the whole relationship depends. Here, in my office, the words "I like you" are the first step towards creating a communion between me and my client. The whole structure of living is based upon what we unconsciously think about, and the values we live by. If the values that we have absorbed from our parents are unhealthy ones, if our unconscious is concentrated upon thoughts of past failures, then we are doomed to repeat those failures again and again. Most people live in a world which is unconscious to them. It is a struggle between the dream of what they would like to be, and the nightmare of what they do to frustrate that dream. That frustration becomes a wall which the client has built between himself and other people, and which he can no longer penetrate. My words dislodge a brick or two from the wall, leaving a hole through which we can look at each other and see if we can like each other. It is my move which makes it possible for us to begin taking down the wall. If I can take his behavior patterns out of his unconscious, and with warmth and a sense of direction bring them into his conscious, then I am giving him a frame of reference. I am offering him a tool for living that will enable him to change his values by living them instead of dreaming about them.

The feeling that one is liked is vital to the development of any human relationship. To love, and to be loved in return, is as much a basic human need as to eat when one is hungry or to drink when one is thirsty. If the physical needs are not fulfilled, the body dies; if the need to give and receive love is not fulfilled, the heart dies. How can one love a person who rejects every expression of one's liking for him? It is natural to want to be liked, to feel that one is worth being liked. But a long series of rejections takes away one's feeling of worth; instead one has the feeling of being "different," unworthy of being liked by other people. Of course, in a world of diverse temperaments and principles and customs, it is not possible to like or be liked by everybody. But each one of us desperately needs to feel that there is one group of people in the world that likes us, that we have one place where we belong and are understood. Most of the people who seek psychotherapy either have lost that place and the feeling that goes with it, or have never felt that they belonged anywhere. They should have had a place in their family, but their family failed them in childhood, through not knowing the difference between rejecting the child, and rejecting its antisocial behavior.

We shall have many hard things to say about parents, who often come close to destroying their children, but those readers who are parents themselves should remember the distinction we have made between dislike and rejection of behavior, and dislike and rejection of a person as a human being. We are involved in a cycle of repeating patterns. Our parents give us feelings of inadequacy and sometimes destroy our happiness because they do not understand the nature of a young child, and how powerful is the effect of their angers, their sly digs, their attitudes. We suffer bitterly from the treatment of our parents, and resolve that our children shall be secure and happy; and so we go about raising our children very differently from the way we were raised, only to find that despite ourselves, the result is the same and the pattern is being repeated. A deep self-knowledge, a deep understanding of what we are doing and why we want to do it, are required to break the pattern. Very few of us have that knowledge or can possibly acquire it without help. I am not joking when I say that nearly every adult in this world badly needs a new education in living. Until the need for it is universally recognized and it is as much a part of our bringing-up as schooling, the children of the future will have no better chance than their parents of growing up as fine human beings who can function at their full potential in every area of their lives.

The recognition that he himself has played some part in producing his unhappy state is the client's first acceptance of emotional responsibility. Entering the therapist's office is his first truly independent action, and is the first step on the road to emotional maturity. Until that moment he had been the slave of his emotions and habit patterns; in crossing the therapist's threshold he raised the flag of rebellion against them, and this act signalled the beginning of a long and bitter struggle, with many battles in different areas. But if he does not give up, he emerges from each battle as a stronger man. The fight never ceases; there is no point at which he will ever again be able to say "I am functioning well enough now; I can stop fighting." There will come a time when he is able to carry on the fight without his therapist's constant advice and support, but unless he is a bigger man than his therapist, he will never be able to say "I have nothing more to learn from him." He will always find something new within himself to question, to accept, or to fight, and new qualities and behavior in other people to observe, to question, and to understand. A good school education stimulates intellectual curiosity and sharpens the mind, but is only the beginning of a process that never stops while the mind is alive. Psychotherapy stimulates emotional curiosity and sharpens the perception of feelings. It is the beginning of an emotional growth that never stops until death. The therapist lives on in the heart of his client, unforgotten, in a way that the schoolmaster does not, unless the relationship to his pupil contained some of the emotional qualities of the therapeutic relationship.

The changes that come about in the client's behavior and personality must inevitably affect his family relationships, because with his growing awareness of people he will see them in a new light, and will react differently to them.

If the parents truly love their child and want him to be happy by living the kind of life he wants to lead, I find that they are understanding and cooperative, and will help the client to carry through any suggestions I make which will help him to grow, especially those concerning higher education or training for the kind of job he wants. Unfortunately such parents are rarely to be found in my office, for the simple reason that their children have been brought up in a loving atmosphere that has guided them towards emotional maturity. Most of the parents whom I meet professionally have not known how to let their children live. Some of them have an inkling of the part they have played in the unhappiness of their children, and gladly admit that they too need my help. Others, however, (and unfortunately they form the majority) say that they love their children, but truly, they have never even known the meaning of the word. Some have smothered their children with a grasping, cloying love, and have ignored their real needs. Others have spent much of their time resenting and evading the emotional demands made on them.

When a client brings his parents to my office, their answer to my request for their help often shocks him, and makes him feel as if the bottom had dropped out of his world. Only recently a young man came to me for help in clearing up the wreckage of a disastrous marriage which had left him feeling no man at all, and for which he had given up his training as an engineer to enter his father's business. In the belief that he had a good relationship with his parents, he brought them to meet me. It had always been his dream to become an engineer, for which his college record showed he had considerable talent, whereas he was unhappy and frustrated in his father's business. He hoped that the plans I had outlined for him to resume his engineering training might induce his father to help him through college. When I requested both their emotional and financial aid for the young man, he saw for the first time what his parents really felt. The father refused point-blank to give any help, because he wanted his son in the business. His mother's sole contribution was: "I always said Martha would leave you." There was no understanding, no constructive idea that would help their son to start his life over again. It was evident that the relationship he had thought so good was really a mockery, and that from childhood his confidence had been undermined by their attitude towards him.

I regard therapy as a process of emotional and social

education, similar to the process that takes place in the socialization of children by their family. The fact that an individual is in conflict with his environment, is to me an indication that he never had an emotionally mature person in his life with whom to identify. Only from a mature person could he have learned the values and the ways of behaving which would ensure that he could love, and express his love; or desire, and fulfill his desires; in a manner which would enrich, rather than impoverish or destroy the other members of the society in which he lives. One of the main functions of parents is to teach the child how to do this, and if their teaching has been inadequate or faulty, the therapist must repair the damage they have done, and complete their work. He must temporarily become a parent-surrogate, fulfilling the functions of a good parent, but the client must eventually be able to see him as a wise friend, an individual in his own right, who is not to be confused emotionally with the biological parent.

Every person who seeks therapy has had difficulty in relating to one parent, or to both. To discover where the trouble lies, we use co-therapists of opposite sex at the client's first interview. Thus, he is immediately thrown into a situation which resembles a family conference. Frequently his first reactions to the combination of male and female therapists quickly reveal the true nature of his problem; if not, the same situation is sustained until the two therapists have gained sufficient information and specific insights. It quickly becomes clear whether the client feels threatened by either of the therapists; he is then placed in the hands of the one with whom he feels safer, that is, to whom he relates with fewer emotional blocks. The other therapist remains in the picture, however, in order to reveal to him many of his habit patterns towards the more "difficult" parent. In the early stages of therapy the mere entry of this therapist into the consulting room can arouse strong emotional reactions in the client; these may then be examined when he is once more alone with his regular therapist. There will eventually come a time when the client is once again able to work with both therapists simultaneously, as at the first interview, or even to work alone with the therapist who has represented the "difficult" parent. This flexible arrangement is constantly adjusted to the immediate needs of the moment. The final aim of the co-therapist relationship is to establish for the client equally healthy patterns with the parent-figure of each sex, and eventually with the biological parents also.

The client often finds, in his relationship with parents and siblings, that they hold back part of their personality, thus depriving him of an essential, sometimes under traumatic circumstances. His therapist, however, is a mature person who brings the whole of his personality to the relationship. Although he is a fallible human being like every other person in this world, he is by the nature of his training in a far better position than most parents to be aware of his client's personal qualities and needs. He cannot, therefore, hold back any part of himself, for in doing so he would be repeating the betrayal his client suffered at the hands of others. He cannot play at being God, or sit upon a pedestal. The client must see the therapist as a man, who can make mistakes but who is capable of loving him with deep understanding and tenderness. I would be bold enough to say that the reason so many therapists do not succeed is that they do not understand the nature of this love; it is not in their own nature. These are the therapists whose patients understand only with their minds the nature of their failings, and can talk easily about their repressions and complexes, but after five years of therapy they still put the blame for their condition entirely on their parents, and have not understood the part they themselves played. The patients may be well adjusted, but they are still incapable of loving, and so are the therapists who treated them. The therapist whose patient leaves him as a mature and loving person, must have brought true love to the relationship; whether he consciously tried to do so, or whether his nature was such that his love made itself felt in spite of the psychoanalytic ritual.

The relationship between the client and his therapist begins as a contract between them; the client is to contribute information about his behavior and feelings, in return for guidance as to how to modify them so that he can function effectively with other people. Supposedly their contributions are to be equal, but during the early stages of therapy the therapist contributes ninety-nine percent and the client only one percent. As the relationship grows, the respective contributions alter, and the relationship then changes in nature as well as in degree, turning from contract into compact. At the beginning it is the therapist who puts the effort into learning about the client, but gradually the client also learns about the therapist, and thereby they come to enrich each other's lives.

In the course of his re-education the client relives many of his past experiences, and attempts to put the therapist into the role of the important figures of his past. But the situations in which the client relives old feelings have actually been created by the therapist, who is aware of what his client is doing and refuses to accept the role thrust upon him. He insists that he is not the client's parent, sibling, mate or lover, but himself. In so doing he makes the client see the situation as it really is, and teaches him to evaluate and react to this reality rather than to the phantom figures and conditions of his past. The client therefore learns to react appropriately to this situation, thus avoiding frustration.

In the first stages of therapy, the therapist's main objective is to break down the defenses of his client and to relieve his anxieties so that he may communicate as freely as possible, because communication is vital. If he cannot express his needs, the therapist cannot help him to fulfill them. He must, therefore, trust the therapist before he can reveal his innermost thoughts and desires. Trust of this kind is not always easy to establish, but it is an essential part of love, and must be established if the therapy is to succeed.

What must we do to bring the first flowering of this trust? In my own view, it is essential that the therapist permit himself to express feeling of warmth towards the client, and never reject the client's expressions of warmth and affection towards him. This does not mean that inappropriate feelings should be indiscriminately expressed on either side. I would say rather that feelings arise from one's perception of a situation. The longer one lives by the values that lead to maturity the more realistically one perceives each situation, and so the less likely it becomes that inappropriate feelings will arise. Warmth and affection are a part of my own nature, and when I meet a client in whom I perceive qualities that I can like and respect, they demand expression. But how can I leave a part of my nature at home? Because I like and respect myself, I can trust myself to express to him the warmth that I feel towards him in any setting where we may meet, in the assurance that it will call forth an appropriate response. It is only the person who feels threatened in his role as a therapist who needs to continue functioning as a therapist when he meets his clients in social settings. If I am secure within myself, I do not need to sit on a pedestal; I can be myself, and not fear to let the client see me function as myself. It is this warmth that lends joy and happiness to my work with people. It is this warmth that first reaches deep into the client and calls up a response from whatever corner of his heart has managed to remain unfrozen.

My expression of warmth is not restricted to my words. Often a glance, a quiet touch of the hand, speaks volumes. The first handshake upon meeting often tells more about a person than half an hour of talk. One who is secure within himself has a quiet, sure way of giving his hand, that conveys immediately his calm confidence in himself. The person who offers you a hand like a dead fish reveals some of his outlook on life, just as the man who pumps your hand up and down shows the lack of confidence for which his boisterous manner is a cover; and the man who squeezes your hand unmercifully (under the impression that he is conveying masculinity) succeeds only in communicating his unexpressed and deep-rooted angers. In the same way, a touch on the shoulder often calms people when they are nervous or crying. It gives them a feeling of belonging, of security, of my personal awareness of them and concern for them. When I first touch a person I always explain what I mean by it, so that he may know what I am doing and distinguishing the feeling behind it. This is necessary, particularly with women, because for some people any physical move is understood as a "bedward" move. Nobody who has been brought up in a family where physical contact is thought to be wrong or undesirable can know, until he is taught, the comfort of a friendly touch where no sexual feeling is involved; the happiness of feeling your brother's arm on your shoulder at a moment of shared joy or sorrow; the strength given off by a father when he has a friendly tussle with his son, or when he takes his daughter on his knee for a bedtime story. All too often I find that behind the confusions of my client lies a family history of giving the child too little love, or else too much love of the wrong kind. In the former case physical contact was not desired; in the latter it was shunned because it was unconsciously desired too much, and was therefore felt to be dangerous. Such persons cannot tell the difference between a friendly gesture and a romantic one. My explanations, therefore, serve a twofold purpose. First, they increase the degree of security he feels with me, because he is given no chance at all to read into my friendly looks and gestures what is not there, or to overlook what is really there. Eventually, when he has come to know me better and explanations are no longer required, my gestures serve as a part of his frame of reference in his relationship to other people. They have added to his vocabulary of feeling, so that his communication with others is increased. In particular, he learns to be sensitive to the feeling that goes with any gesture, so that he no longer reacts inappropriately to physical contact. Sooner or later my expressions of warmth, both in words and gestures, call up a response in the client. It may not at first be direct, but it is reflected in the way he looks, the way he holds himself, in his words, all expressing his faith in me.

There have been occasional cases where no expression of warmth, no word or gesture or deed, has been able to awaken any positive response at all, and indeed where I have met only with complete rejection. In such cases, where any expression of warmth is basically unacceptable to the person, I cannot work with him. I will not be robbed of my right to express my true nature, which includes a genuine affection towards everybody in whom I can find even a single quality to like and respect. The person who flatly rejects warmth, and refuses to give or receive it, is a person who wants to stay sick and is willing to pay for the privilege of doing so, and perhaps of hurting or destroying the therapist in the process. I will sell my time, but not my soul, and for me to attempt to treat anyone who is that sick *would* be selling my soul. Resistance of that nature is testing the weakness of the therapist, and I want no part of it. There are plenty of unhappy people in the world who want to get rid of their unhappiness, and find a channel through which they can allow their fine qualities to emerge from the prison which their bad habit patterns have created around them. These are the people that I treat. These are the people who have secretly longed to be able to love, and to give, and yet have been unable to do so. These are the people whose deep wish it is to create, and who hate themselves because they know they are destructive in spite of their wish. I can help such people, because I can find the good in them that can be cherished and nursed to strength. But I will not bring destruction down upon my own head by becoming involved with those who wish only to destroy, nor will I expose my other clients to this danger.

I am bound to set limits on the kind of person that

The Client-Therapist Relationship

I undertake to work with, because my colleagues and I do not work in isolation, keeping our clients separated from one another. We are educators, not clinical psychologists, and our educational method demands that the therapists and all their clients be welded into one therapeutic community. We believe that psychotherapy is an education in living, which operates by the substitution of good habit patterns for bad ones. Therapy is part of the stream of living, not something outside it. We wish to observe how the client reacts in certain situations, and also to allow him to perceive his own reactions at the time they occur. We want to teach him how to build relationships of a kind he has never before experienced. And so we throw all these people, of very diverse temperament, into close contact with each other. Thus we have a little world within the world. It is protected by the vigilance of the therapist, but it is also in close contact with the larger world. We can create whatever situations we desire, because in such a mixed collection of people there are bound to arise loves, jealousies, happiness, successes, angers, and indeed every basic emotion and situation that occurs between humans. We can stimulate reactions in our clients by asking two people who appear to be antagonistic to spend some time in each other's company. If both of them frequently discuss the relationship with their therapists to gain a better understanding of each other, they may become friends. At worst they will remain antagonistic, but having learned a great deal about themselves before they part company. But it is the protection that I want to stress, as well as the learning. In our protected setting basically nice people can quarrel and fight, and learn to be less destructive while doing so. But I must provide full protection. I cannot afford to let loose a tiger among those who trust me, and that is why I will not work with a person who really wishes to destroy either himself or others. Sad to say, there are such people, but my office is no place for them, and even orthodox psychiatrists have to beware of them.

I have said that the people who come to me for help are those who have wanted to love and to give, but have not known how. Everything I have spoken of so far is a part of knowing how to love. But a healthy love is always an exchange, and it is in this matter of giving and receiving that people often have the most difficulty. Giving and receiving is often tied up with unhealthy patterns acquired early in childhood. Christ said, "It is more blessed to give than to receive," but this saying is all too often misunderstood. It is only true when the feeling that goes with the gift is a healthy one. The material object is only a symbol of your feeling, and this in turn is one part of an exchange. Your gift is the sign of the warm feelings that overflow from your heart, and these are the response to the happiness you have had from the person to whom you are giving. When the feelings are natural and spontaneous and are a healthy response, you never stop to think "Now I really *must* send something to Paul." The trouble is that naturalness and spontaneity depend almost entirely upon understanding the other person's needs and what gives him pleasure. This awareness does not come naturally; it has to be learned. In the beginning it is the result of a conscious study and effort. But when awareness of other people has become as automatic a part of your functioning as breathing or walking, and when you can trust your feelings as a good guide to conduct, then the impulse to give also becomes spontaneous, and the manner in which the gift is presented becomes a true expression of your feelings. At this level you find the seeming paradox, that sometimes your finest gift is to do nothing, except allow your friend the freedom to give to you. With giving, as with any other action, it is your motivation that counts for everything; if the motivation is good, the results will be good.

The people who come to see me have never learned to examine their own motivations and those of other people. As children they indeed learned to "fear the Greeks when they bring gifts," because children have not learned to use words to hide their thoughts. They penetrate surely and swiftly right through words and actions to the feelings that lie behind. When presents are showered on them they look for the feelings underneath, and if these are not loving, they come to distrust gifts. They associate receiving presents with uncomfortable feelings, and so they become equally chary of giving them.

Take a look at Pamela, for example. Pamela's mother was a woman who had a great contempt for men and was very insecure in all her personal relationships. She constantly tried to cover up these insecurities by making herself indispensable to her family. Any new or unfamiliar situation was a source of worry, and she could trust nobody to be loving and decent. Her friends were constantly "letting her down," and every merchant was a potential robber. Her only security was in dominating her family so that they always did exactly what she wanted. There was only one way of doing anything—her way. Pamela was a child of unusual talent with a mind of her own, and became a severe threat to her mother, who proceeded to undermine Pamela's confidence in herself as a person. If Pamela found her own way of doing anything, it was no good. If she rebelled against her mother's domination, she was odd. Her mother constantly made her of no account in front of family and friends. And yet Pamela's mother would speak in honeyed tones about the joys of giving presents and making people happy, and how she had done so much for her family. It is small wonder that the shower of presents made Pamela feel desperately that they were just something else she was supposed to be grateful for, and that the gifts were a further demand that she do what her mother wanted. She knew, deep down, that her mother did not love her, but she tried desperately, and without success, to win the love she needed. Her mother's gifts to her were demands for submission, and hers to her mother were pleas for a love that she knew she could not obtain. In the end she stopped giving, because gifts meant nothing to her and contained no love. She also pushed aside those from other people, being quite unable to receive them gracefully, and so she was labeled "ungrateful" and "heartless."

Some people give because they want something in return; others, in order to show how rich or clever they are. Giving allows them to feel superior to other people, and so they will never accept anything in return. Still others send a gift to someone they dislike, "because Aunt Mary sent us that flower vase, and whatever will she think if we don't send her something?" Shops and advertisers cash in on Christmas, Father's Day, Mother's Day, birthdays, anniversaries and so on, to the point where it has become a social obligation to give something to almost all your acquaintances, whether you like them or not. The people I work with need to learn the meaning of a gift all over again. And so in order to help them feel that they belong, that I am concerned for them, that their struggles to acquire self-respect and respect for others arouse my admiration and bring me happiness; I give them some material gift that I know will please them, as soon as I am sure that they will understand the feelings that go with it. And if they bring me flowers or other presents I do not refuse them, because I know that these are the first expressions of a real feeling of warmth toward me that spring from an appreciation of what they have learned during our session.

The most valuable gift, however, is the intangible one of understanding, of shared feelings, of time and effort spent on your friend's behalf; that looks for no return, but is given out of your affection for him and because his happiness is yours also. A look or a touch on the arm is not only a communication; it is a gift of part of yourself. Asking a friend to help you is also a gift to him, because it tells him, better than words, that you trust him and like him.

There is an old Basque proverb that runs: " 'Take what you want,' says God, 'Take it and pay for it.' " Whatever you take, there is a price to pay. If what you want is not in accordance with your real needs, unhappiness is that price. But if happiness is what you want, you can get it only through other people, who accord you respect, a sense of your worth, and the feeling that you are valued by them. The only currency in which you can pay for that happiness is the personal effort you put into understanding them. What they do for you will, if you let it, fill your pass on that happiness to others. This kind of happiness comes unbidden, and cannot be hoarded for your own secret enjoyment. In giving, as in all other aspects of love, you must hold your friend close with open hands.

> Who binds unto himself a joy,
> Doth the winged life destroy;
> But he that catches the joy as it flies
> Lives in eternity's sunrise.*

Learning to catch the joy as it flies, how to hold close with open hands, is a very important part of what the therapist has to teach his client.

* William Blake

Chapter III

THE CLIENT

Almost every client is very self-involved when he first enters therapy. He reacts to the people and events in his world only as they affect him personally, and since his view of any situation is apt to be highly distorted, the results are often distressing to him. He is generally obsessed by some problem that appears so pressing and yet so insurmountable that it overshadows everything else. As an extreme illustration, let me tell you about Tommy. I had scheduled his second appointment for Friday morning, but on Wednesday afternoon he entered the reception room and sat down, speaking to no one. After about five minutes he suddenly jumped up, and knocked loudly on the door of my room, where a therapists' conference was in progress. Receiving no answer, he pounded on the door and walked in before anyone had time to reply. Threading his way through the therapists, he reached my desk and leaned over it, saying:

"Dr. List, I just *have* to talk to you; I have a terrible problem." I had already heard from his sister what was on Tommy's mind, and knew that it could wait, so I answered gently:

"I know, Tommy, but let's wait and talk about it on Friday when you come for your appointment—I have problems too, you know." And I waved my hand at my colleagues. Then, smiling, I added "Maybe we'll talk about my problems too when you come in; you might be able to help me." He looked at me, very surprised, and replied:

"I don't suppose there will be much of my hour left for that—*my* problem is *really serious.*"

Not all my clients allow their problems to lead them into such discourtesy, but every one feels to some degree that *his* problem is the most important one in the world, and so he is bound to have a certain disregard for other people's feelings and convenience. We expect this, for the new client is confused, lonely and rather frightened. He brings with him to the first therapeutic session a lifetime of frustrations, unhappiness and bad experiences, and expects the therapist, in one hour, to settle his unhappy existence for him. The specific problem which the new client presents to his therapist is very seldom his most serious one. He may, for example, tell the therapist that he is unhappy in his marriage, but he does not yet realize that the core of his problem is his own low opinion of himself. This opinion is often unrealistic, based on distorted ideas about his own strengths and weaknesses, but he inevitably communicates it to other people in all sorts of ways. Because he feels worthless, he constantly maneuvers himself into positions that prove his inadequacy. He certainly does not behave this way on purpose, and usually does not even realize what he is doing. His unconscious, with its nagging whisper, "I am no good, I am a failure, I am rotten," makes him overlook or misinterpret the real facts of every situation, so that he inevitably behaves as he thinks a "no-good rotten failure" would behave. The man who sees himself as a slob invites all the world to treat him as a slob.

Because the client's attitude towards himself so powerfully affects his behavior, the therapist using the List Method does not dwell upon the original problem, which is seldom more than a symptom. He regards discussion of this problem only as a means of gaining information about the ways in which the person's self-concept is distorted. Dwelling on the problem itself would give too much importance not only to the symptom, but to the negative thinking associated with it. After two or three sessions, therefore, the therapist quietly diverts his client's attention away from the sick area, and concentrates upon finding and strengthening healthy areas. The client is kept so busy trying new behavior patterns which will allow him to respect himself, that one day he discovers his original problem has quietly disappeared, or, if it is still there, that he has at least gained some of the insight and strength which will enable him to solve it for himself in due course. *This is what I call substituting a program for a problem.*

One youngster came to us complaining that he did not know how to talk to girls, and that all his unhappiness stemmed from the fact that no girl would go out with him twice because he bored them so much on the first date. Bobby's real problem was that his brilliant brother had always overshadowed him, and his family had made him feel a failure by comparison. In fact, Bobby was intelligent, loving by nature, and had several useful talents, but his sense of inadequacy kept him stagnating in a dead-end job. His therapist concentrated upon developing these talents, getting him back to school, and encouraging him to move in circles where his qualities would be appreciated. For a few sessions he would constantly complain:

"But you aren't telling me how to talk to girls!"

To which his therapist would reply:

"Never mind the girls right now. You're doing fine. Concentrate on getting this new job which is going to give you the money to go back to school—that's far more important."

So Bobby would give his therapist a reproachful look, but he stopped griping about girls and worked on the tasks at hand. After he had been in therapy about six months he made another effort to extract the secret of talking to girls. He got the shock of his life when his therapist turned round and said to him:

"If you're so bad at talking to girls, how come you managed to have three of them splitting their sides laughing while you described your hitchhiking adventures last night? And how come Irene told me she spent a wonderful evening with you last week, and asked me when you were going to invite her out again?"

Bobby's jaw dropped in astonishment, and he said thoughtfully:

"That's right; I *can* talk to girls, after all. It doesn't seem so difficult any more."

His program had greatly altered his feeling about himself. He was gaining self-respect and learning to have fun at the same time. He was no longer a bore, but was becoming a lively and interesting young man.

This description of Bobby's case has had to be oversimplified in order to make the point. What I did not mention was the very hard work put in by both Bobby and his therapist in order to get him to the point where his initial problem had vanished. I did not tell you of the patience and love of his therapist; nor of Bobby's repeated efforts, and often his repeated failures, to make one step forward; of the moments when he gained an insight into the motivations underlying some of his actions and words, or how searingly painful to him some of those insights were. But the thought that he could be master of himself and lead the kind of life he wanted, combined with the trust he placed in his therapist, sustained him through painful times and were vital preliminaries to the moment when he could say: "That's right; I *can* talk to girls, after all."

Bobby has found that being able to talk to girls is by

no means all that he wants from life. He knows much more about himself, but also knows that he has still more to learn. He is well launched on his first program, and when he has achieved its primary goals he will extend it towards higher goals. He will never feel that he is without a purpose in life, and will always be learning more effectively how to live each day to the full, so that when he goes to bed at night he can look back upon a day that has been rich in experience, and satisfying to him. His life will have become his program.

I always stress the importance of higher education as a vital part of the program, because I have found that most people can benefit enormously from it, both materially and emotionally. We substitute a program for the client's problem, but it must not be supposed that this is a matter of handing the client a ready-made blueprint for his life. On the contrary, his program must evolve naturally from his own dreams of what he wants to do with his life. It must be geared realistically to his capabilities, and must meet his individual needs. An educational program, however, is almost universally the best point at which to start the client in his new way of life. In many cases he is earning his living in an occupation which is unsatisfactory and distasteful to him; if he is to break away and venture into a new and more congenial profession, then he must be equipped for the task. Even if he likes his current profession, and wishes to stay in it, additional qualifications will certainly increase his status. Some of our young clients have no clear idea of how they can best use their interests and talents. In such cases the discipline of an educational program often serves to clarify their thinking and by the time they have come to a decision, they are already some way along the road towards obtaining the qualifications they need.

The psychological benefits of an educational program are even greater than the material ones. The new problems involved in deciding upon the field of study, in raising the money required, and in organizing his life to make time for studying, all distract his attention from the neurotic problem that brought him to me. The first steps may present him with both material and emotional difficulties, but his therapist shows him that he is capable of solving these problems. Their solution gives him a measure of confidence, and sets a pattern of success which is particularly important for his future growth. The client's opinion of himself is immediately raised by the knowledge that someone whom he trusts believes him capable of achieving a degree.

When I speak about the client's "self-concept," I am not referring to his *conscious* thoughts about himself. Many a man at first impresses his colleagues as a tough, hardboiled character, who thinks highly of himself, is competent in his work, confident in his ability, and well on the road to success. Larry is such a man, but when we probe deeper we find that he is using these exterior qualities, which impress other people, as a cover for deep-seated insecurities. He *has* to appear confident, lest others should uncover the weaknesses in himself that he dimly suspects, but dares not face. At some period of his childhood, Larry's parents made him feel that he was a disappointment to them, that he was inadequate in some vital area. Not that they told him explicitly that he was no good, they loved him too much for that; but nothing that he ever did received their warm approval. There was always the feeling that he had failed them in some way. When he was a small boy Larry felt that the only way he could gain his parents' love was to *prove* to them that he could live up to their hopes for him. He has been doing just that, ever since. They implanted in him a doubt that he was worthy of their love, and it penetrated so deeply that even their death could not stop his need to go on proving his worth. Anyone who in speech, or manner, or status, reminds Larry of his father, at once loses his own identity. One tone of voice that recalls his childhood, and Larry is lost. His eyes register the features of his friend, but the picture never reaches his mind. That tone has reawakened old feelings that scream inside him: "Father is angry—he doesn't love me any more—I've disappointed him again." The fears and angers of the past have taken control once more, and Larry's subsequent actions, though they may appear logical, are basically designed to placate a man who has been dead for ten years, instead of being a healthy response to a present friend.

St. Paul wrote to the Corinthians: "When I was a child, I spake as a child, I understood as a child, I thought as a child, but when I became a man I put away childish things. For now we see through a glass, darkly, but then face to face; now I know in part, but then I shall know even as also I am known." * He was speaking of man's progress towards the knowledge of God, but we can also apply his words to our progress towards knowledge of ourselves. The people who come to my office still see themselves and the world "through a glass, darkly." They have not known how to remove the glass, nor has anyone helped them to do so. They have been unable to put away the fears and angers of childhood, because though they have acquired the language and the responsibilities of men, emotionally they still understand as children.

When I speak of "knowing ourselves," I am well aware that I am treading on ground that for centuries has been hotly disputed by philosophers and theologians. What *is* this "self" that we are to know? Once we start exploring this field, we find so many conflicting theories that it is impossible even to outline them here, nor is it necessary. In my work I am concerned with teaching people how to live. In other words, I am concerned with their behavior. Experience has convinced me that our behavior is governed by what we *think* we are in comparison with other human beings. In my practice, therefore, I work with the client's self-concept, which I can reach and modify, rather than with the psyche, or soul, which is beyond my grasp. I define the self-concept as the *sum of the thoughts and feelings, both conscious and unconscious, which make up the individual's concept of who and what he is.*

* I Corinth., xiii, 11-12.

The self-concept is learned. Everything that one knows and feels about himself is derived from his experiences in life, with social experiences being of major importance. There is no point in an individual's life at which his self-concept becomes completely stabilized, in the sense that it is no longer subject to change. It is continually being modified as the result of interaction with the environment, though it must be remembered that such interaction can affect only certain parts of the self-concept at any one time. Furthermore, it is chiefly those areas which have been most recently established which are most easily changed. Those parts which were established early in childhood, and were reinforced over a period of years, are extremely resistant to change. For this reason the self-concept strives to maintain itself against the influence of the environment. There is a marked consistency in every individual's behavior even though he may see himself as inferior to others. He resists strongly anything which is incompatible with his own set of values, distorted though these may be. What little evidence he sees of his worth and capability is comparatively powerless against the deep feeling of worthlessness that has persisted since childhood.

Whenever the individual feels threatened, his resistance to change is very greatly increased, and his behavior becomes extremely rigid. On the other hand, in an environment which does not threaten him he can be induced to reach out for new experiences. The more mature person affirms his value and worth as a unique human being, and because he trusts his ability to assess both the facts and the emotional tone of any situation, his behavior is a true expression of his self-concept. He knows his needs, his strengths and his limitations, and has a set of values and ideals by which to govern his conduct. He strives always to satisfy his needs in accordance with his values. He is self-directed and flexible.

However, when an individual's perceptions are distorted, his judgment is clouded. The direction of his conduct is then left to his pride, his impulses, his conscience, his deep-rooted fears and anxieties. When choices for action arise, such a person is unable to recognize his true needs, or to perceive the demands of the situation correctly. He therefore frequently experiences a conflict between what he really wants to do and what he believes he ought to do. Implicitly, such a person distrusts both his feelings and his intellectual abilities as guides to his conduct. Instead of striving to develop both his emotional and intellectual capacities and to bring them into harmony, he habitually follows some inflexible moral code or some stringent ideals to which he believes he must conform at all costs. The net consequence is that in the eyes of society he may behave in a moral and exemplary fashion, but his real needs are ignored and he will be perpetually frustrated.

At the beginning of his quest for self-knowledge, nearly every client feels that by watching other people he will know what to think of himself, because he thinks they see him objectively and therefore react according to what they see. This belief is mistaken, and puts the cart before the horse. Few people in fact see him objectively or penetrate much below the surface. They react only to his behavior, which is governed by what he *unconsciously* feels about himself as well as by his conscious thoughts and desires. If his security in his own worth was damaged as a child, there is a conflict between the picture of himself that he wishes to project and his true feelings about himself. This conflict continually directs his behavior towards trying to conceal what he considers to be his weaknesses. As long as he does not admit the weaknesses to himself and learn to deal with them, he is vulnerable to anyone who cares to probe and use them. Furthermore, it is not only traits of character that we have to face and accept, but our physical traits also. Almost everybody thinks he has a physical defect. We have a mole on our cheek, or a couple of freckles, or too large a nose, or ears that stick out too far, or a few pounds too much fat, and hate ourselves for this defect. Usually it was painfully drawn to our attention in childhood or adolescence, and thereafter nobody could convince us that a trait which we consider repulsive does not prevent other people from loving us. Often we cling to our fat or our ugly nose in order to have something tangible to blame for our unhappiness, instead of facing the fact that we can and should make changes in our behavior.

It is of the utmost importance that the client should learn to like and respect himself, and to behave in such a way as to maintain his self-respect. When he can do so, he also knows how to protect himself and is no longer vulnerable to attack from malicious or jealous people. He may suffer disappointment or bereavement, but because neither attack nor grief can any longer threaten his sense of worth or his survival, he can adapt his behavior to take into account the new situations they create. The child who quakes before the teacher, the woman who lets her grocer cheat her, the man who permits his boss to make fun of him, all desire this control. Unfortunately without skilled help from a mature person, few of us are able to attain it because we become too involved with our own problems to make the effort to solve them.

We teach the client to concentrate on changing the habit patterns that he does not like, and learning what his limitations are and how to live with them, so that he will no longer spend time brooding over the faults of others. It is very easy for him to say "It was *his* fault, not mine," or "I don't like him," but the mature individual does not waste his time in such trivialities. Instead he looks within himself to discover the reasons for his dislike and for the other person's reactions, acknowledging the possibility that he himself may be in the wrong and may need to make changes in his own outlook and behavior. When the client understands that his behavior patterns are influenced by his self-concept, he can make changes in his behavior. He begins to accept new values, and to form a picture of how a person behaves who lives by those values. Gradually, as he stabilizes new and healthy habit patterns, his actual self concept in those areas begins to approach the ideal that he has formulated.

Some people believe that to be unhappy is an abnormal state. I do not believe this to be true. Certainly it is abnormal to be unhappy most of the time and to accept this unhappiness without attempting to change it; just as a continually euphoric state would be abnormal. A normal life contains both unhappiness and joy. Joy is an active emotion, not the passive acceptance of the absence of unhappiness. Joy is an affirmation. It is saying "Yes" to life with all its experiences. It comes unbidden, but only to the man of integrity who is willing to make evaluations, choose what he believes to be good and fight for it with all his energies. Such a man will not accept the second-rate. To him, unhappiness is the awareness that he is not using all his energies and talents to their full extent. It is this kind of unhappiness that can be used therapeutically as an irritant, for every client needs something to fight if he is to grow. There is no such thing as easy progress in self-knowledge.

If a man is unhappy in his job, then he wishes to change it and find another that will offer him more satisfaction. Whether his therapist will allow him to do so or not, is another matter. He will not allow his client to suffer unnecessary frustration for long, but it may so happen that frustration arises from his inability to handle the personal relationships involved, rather than from the work itself. In that case the therapist often advises his client to stay on his job, and concentrates upon helping him to handle the personal side. When he can handle this adequately, but finds that the work itself does not offer him enough scope, then he has made a step forward and is ready to move on to another job. The therapist has used both positive and negative sides of the situation to induce a change in the client's behavior. On the one hand, an irritant was administered by keeping the client in a situation which was unpleasant to him; on the other hand, there was the implication that staying and mastering the situation which was unpleasant to him would produce increased happiness. But the very fact of mastering this situation alters the client's opinions about what he can be and do, and increases his confidence in himself, so that the reasons for which he does in fact leave the job are very different, and much healthier, than those for which he originally wished to leave it.

We once had a client who wanted a college degree to improve her professional position. Obtaining this degree was very important to her, but she was having great difficulty in college because her school experiences had been unfortunate, and she felt deep down that really, she was stupid. It took her almost seven years to complete her college education, because her pattern of behavior was to run away from the situation the moment that she felt threatened. What generally happened to Judy was that she would attend classes regularly until the mid-term examinations loomed ahead. During this time she made a very good impression upon her classmates and professors, who admired her grasp of the subject material and her stimulating contributions to classroom discussions.

89

However, written examinations were anathema to Judy, and for a week beforehand she would be in a state of mounting panic, until on the day itself she would completely break down and fail to attend school. Once she had missed the examination she would then be afraid to return, so she would cut school for the remainder of the term and be dropped from the course. Judy's therapist was well aware of her pattern and of her self-concept in the scholastic area. By his work with her in other areas, and by arranging special coaching from instructors with whom she felt secure and who were able to reach her on an emotional as well as an academic level, he gradually built up her strength, so that each new term found her a little stronger and more confident than the one before. Because Judy felt completely accepted by him, she was finally able to go to him well before the examination and admit her fears. This verbal admission freed Judy from her old pattern of running away from the situation. Her therapist accepted this, as he had accepted everything else about her, and suggested ways in which she might be helped. Since her energies were no longer tied up in concealing the fear, she was able to accept that she was capable of succeeding in college, and that her fears were unrealistic. In the remaining time before the mid-term, her therapist and her friends gave her constant moral support and help in her work. Two of her friends escorted her to school on the day of the examination, and waited to take her home. These preparations bore fruit, for when she entered the examination room she found that though nervous, she was able to summon enough strength to answer the easiest of the questions without difficulty. After that, the answers to the other questions came flooding into her mind, and she received a B grade in every subject. Now she knew that she was capable of completing her education. Three years after breaking the pattern, Judy held both the B.A. and M.A. degrees and had found the employment she had long desired.

It is through the therapist that the client begins to visualize his self-concept and its relation to his behavior patterns. The individual's self awareness is stimulated from the beginning of his treatment by the positive comments his therapist makes about him. He begins to see himself through his therapist's realistic eyes. The therapist may remark to a woman that she has a very soft, feminine look about her. It might also be true that her style of clothing is unbecoming—but the therapist does not remark about this. Another time he might comment on her perception of other people's feelings. Since these remarks are made with sincerity the client unconsciously responds to them, and although she is unaware of it, her self-concept is slightly improved because of the new confidence she has gained.

Nearly every client who has a low self-concept feels at a disadvantage in social gatherings. His earlier bad experiences at such events cause him to fear them. He is afraid that the painful situations which arose in the past will repeat themselves, and this very fear not only prevents him from enjoying himself, but actually does bring about their repetition. One individual may withdraw completely from the activities and hover uncertainly in a corner throughout the evening. Another is not able to function without drinking heavily. The effects of this heavy drinking often prove most embarrassing to him after the party. Still another feels that he cannot function at gatherings unless he becomes the center of attention; he tells off-color jokes in a loud voice, or insists upon playing practical jokes, or exhibiting fancy dance routines, in a manner which tends to make others uncomfortable.

Each new party presents a threat to these individuals and it becomes increasingly difficult for them to attend. They are afraid of parties but they cannot analyze their fear. Sometimes they make excuses to themselves that the parties are dull, or that others are not considerate of them —but they still attend, often out of a sense of obligation to the hostess. The effects of these parties have severely damaged their self-concepts. The withdrawn individual retreats further into his shell; the boisterous person becomes louder; the show-off more obnoxious. They cannot help themselves.

One part of the List Method is the education the clients receive in the proper behavior at social gatherings. This offers them the opportunity to learn what their behavior is; what frightens them about social situations; and how to change their behavior so that they will feel free to enjoy themselves. My wife and I arrange three major social events a year for my clients; a New Year's Eve party, our birthday party in June, and a Thanksgiving party which also celebrates our wedding anniversary. The members of the various groups also give parties during the year, but on a smaller scale.

Since the three major parties are so spread throughout the year, the new client is invited to attend one of them within a few months of beginning therapy. He faces it with all of his old feelings about social events, and his behavior at the party is the same as it has been in the past. This gives both his therapist and himself the opportunity to see how he functions. If his social behavior is inconsiderate or offensive he feels it in the reaction of the other clients. The results of this party are very different from all the others he has attended, because people point out to him the exact manner in which he has offended. After one party, for example, Janine learned for the first time why women avoided her, when it was pointed out to her that she had made passes at a married man during the evening. Janine had been unaware of what she was doing and of the effects it had upon her friends, because in the past no one had reproached her or pointed out the specific ways in which she had given offense.

Since acceptance is the important catalyst for this period of evaluation, the client is able to admit that his old patterns of behavior are undesirable both to himself and to others. As he gains assurance of his acceptance and as the members of his group reach out to include him or to help him feel at ease, he is able to relax and enjoy the parties. In time he becomes able to do the same for other members with a similar problem. Thus, through the consideration he receives and gives, he is able to change his mode of social behavior, and this improves his self-concept.

Unhealthy relationships with authority figures are another frequent source of damage to the self-concept. Although the client may be unaware of it, most of the patterns of behavior which he exhibits with authority figures were established during his childhood, and are no longer appropriate. When the individual and the authority figure are of the same sex, the pattern of behavior is one of competition. Ann had held five different jobs of a responsible nature in the period of a year, and had either been fired or had resigned in anger over a small incident —always blaming her boss for her troubles. After an examination of her employment problem she was able to see that it was she herself who had set up the unpleasant situations. Ann had always been in competition with her mother and repeated this pattern whenever she was employed by a woman, competing with her boss to prove that she could do the job better. Each time she competed with her mother she was punished by the withdrawal of love; each time she competed on the job she was fired. As a result her concept of herself as a woman was severely distorted.

Extreme humility is another form which the behavior pattern may take. Many individuals allow others to walk all over them because they are afraid to assert themselves. They are the ones who are regarded as "slobs" and people either take advantage of them or avoid them because their "nothingness" causes others to feel uncomfortable. An example of this is the gangster's stooge who humbles himself constantly in order to curry favor with the chief. This is usually done for one of two reasons. First, the individual may feel he is really better than the authority but is afraid of this feeling. He therefore buries it, and humbles himself so that the authority will not discover it. Second, the individual may actually be frightened, because he feels the authority has some power which will harm him, and he therefore humbles himself so that the "kind parent" will not beat the "little child."

A third form which the behavior pattern may take is active rebellion. The individual may feel so threatened by authority that he rebels against every suggestion, expression, or order. There is much in the literature on juvenile delinquency about the pattern of active rebellion. People who constantly rebel against the conventions and laws of our society often do it out of anger at the authority which society in general represents. Their fight is really within themselves, but they take the easier way of "solving" things by striking out at something intangible rather than seeking out the roots of their problem and dealing with themselves. No matter which pattern of behavior the individual uses with authority-figures, his self-concept is greatly damaged and he is unhappy in each situation.

The client's behavior with authorities is first seen at the beginning of his relationship with his therapist. Many attempt to make the therapist a god, a family member, or the boss. The therapist needs to be constantly aware of this and must consistently try to prevent the client from seeing him as one of the figures of the client's past. This is one of the major reasons that the List Method stresses the very great importance of observing the therapist in as many types of life situations as possible. It is easier for the client to see the therapist as another human being with his own problems, if he sees that the therapist has the same needs and problems as himself, but also sees him handling them in a more mature manner.

The group members in the therapeutic community also play a very important part in helping the client to deal with authority-figures. An authority-figure is not always a person in authority, but is often a person endowed by the client with some power which the individual does not really have. As the client develops relationships he learns to identify the type of person to whom he has previously been unable to relate. When he makes a serious effort to develop a relationship with such individuals he begins to understand many of his problems with authority-figures, and since the group has his interest at heart, they help him to gain an understanding of his behavior with this type of person and of the unconscious motivations behind it. Once these are understood, he becomes able to relate to such individuals.

The result of working through the problems raised by the client's program is a change in his self-concept. He begins to acquire a sense of identity, and begins to perceive his specific strengths and weaknesses. He becomes capable of building up his strengths, and of eliminating

weak points or turning them to advantage. Many a weakness can be changed into a strength. Ira, for example, was
a man of compulsive orderliness who could not bear un-
tidiness or inefficiency of any sort. As a result of a suggestion from his therapist, he left the frustrating work he
was engaged in, and obtained a position as assistant to
an industrial executive. Here he was in his element; he
was responsible for the detailed execution of the broad
plans outlined by the executives, who hated to be bothered
with details. He also found a creative outlet, since he was
in a position to know which departments were functioning with less than maximum efficiency, and he delighted
in creating highly detailed plans for reorganizing such
departments. As a result, production was increased con-
siderably without extra burden on the operatives, and
because Ira had found a useful and creative outlet for his
orderly instincts, they ceased to be compulsive. He could
therefore tolerate in his home the comfortable disorder
which two young children leave in their wake, but which
had once driven him to distraction.

Chapter IV

GROUP PSYCHOTHERAPY

Man is essentially a gregarious animal, whose strength, and indeed whose very survival, depends largely upon his ability to form groups having a common purpose. Every man is born into a family group, and our highly complex culture imposes upon him an ever expanding participation in groups of various kinds. The very fact of being born into our society will eventually entail certain responsibilities, such as paying his federal taxes (at the national level), or teaching his children how to behave (at the family level). In addition, he will probably take on membership of other groups by his own choice—recreation groups, political groups, work groups. The isolated man is cut off from any interchange of ideas or sharing of feelings, and thereby loses some of his humanity. His capacity for emotional or spiritual growth is limited in

99

proportion to the degree and duration of his solitude.

Many of the roles in which we find ourselves are indissolubly connected with several overlapping groups. The father is also a son, and a husband, and is thus a member of two kinship groups in addition to being the head of his own family. The role of a mother is not confined to her relations with her children, but extends into membership of other groups in the community, such as the PTA. In his pre-school years the child will probably be a member of a loosely-knit group of friends of his own age, but from the moment that he enters school he becomes a member of a highly structured group outside the family, that of his school class. And so the child, as he grows, gradually participates in the functioning of more and more groups, some of them very loosely-knit, some of them very highly structured. It is the individual's pattern of behavior in his family that determines how he will function in other groups. The person who from early childhood has experienced family unity, has seen his parents working together, and has been taught and encouraged to cooperate with them, will have learned the basic responsibilities and privileges of group membership. If he never learns to share a task with his parents, or to take minor responsibilities in the family such as small chores that smooth the running of the household, then he is likely to find it very hard to cooperate with others later in life. All his successes and failures in relation to groups in the outside world, are extensions of his successes and failures in his own family group.

Group Psychotherapy

The List Method makes extensive use of group situations to educate the client in areas where his family experiences left much to be desired. Group psychotherapy is widely used in other settings, but usually as an alternative to individual therapy. We have found that the two forms of therapy enhance each other, and that the use of both together greatly accelerates the client's growth.

If we are to understand what a therapeutic group is, and what forces are at work in it, we should first clarify what we mean by a "group." What is it, for instance, that differentiates a collection of men and women with varying degrees of acquaintance meeting in the therapeutic setting, from a carful of people riding the subway to the race-track? One might first suggest that a group is any collection of individuals who meet at a given time and place for the same reasons. It is true that a common purpose is one element that goes into making a group. But it is not the whole answer. The people in the subway car, for instance, all intend to watch the races and perhaps play the horses, but this is not enough to induce them to talk very much, if they encounter and recognize each other later in the day. The fact that those particular people are in that particular car is something of an accident; they did not arrange to meet each other, and they will separate once they reach the race-track. The people in the subway car are, in fact, a collection of individuals pursuing their individual ends. If we can look at the problem a little differently, and see that having similar individual goals

101

is not by any means the same thing as sharing a common purpose, we are within sight of the key to the problem. Let us take a look, for example, at the Board of Directors of Shepherd & Woolgatherer, Inc. Its members have a number of similar individual goals. Each wants to make money, to be loved by his family, to feel that his life has purpose and that his work makes sense; but to achieve these goals it is not necessary for them to meet at all. However, they also share a common purpose, which is to increase the sales of Shepherd & Woolgatherer. They may all have different ideas on how this is to be done. But if the ideas are to be translated into action that will further the common purpose, they must be brought out into the open and discussed. It is this exchange of ideas and of feelings, this sustained and active intention of communicating, that welds a collection of individuals into a group.

Once a group has been formed, many forces come into play. Some are cohesive, and tend to bind individual members more closely to the group; others are disruptive, tending to drive the members out of the group. The feeling of any member towards the group is determined by the balance of these forces. The cohesiveness of the whole group, that is, its strength and its "we-feeling," is the sum of all the forces acting on all the members to keep them in the group.

Every group sets itself a task or goal of some kind. The ultimate goal of each member of a therapeutic group is to get well. He wishes to learn what prevents him from functioning adequately in the three major areas of life —occupational, social, and sexual. More simply: he wants to learn how to live, instead of just existing.

Each member of the group has had trouble with interpersonal relationships. The basis of the trouble has in most cases been their inability to recognize and communicate their true feelings. Therefore, one of the two major goals of the therapeutic group is maximum communication between the members. Before one can verbalize an emotion, he must first recognize it. The group often helps him by identifying it for him, and telling him how he is expressing it. His words are seldom important, for emotions are conveyed far more strongly by his physical aspect and actions. The language of the body is eloquent, and reveals to the alert observer what the subject can conceal even from his own consciousness. Sweet words are belied by the edge in the speaker's voice which often deals a more deadly blow than open anger. A gruff voice can try to cover warm feelings, though seldom effectively. The tension of fear or insecurity is conveyed by body posture or small movements, however calm the voice; anger may be betrayed by a swift tightening of the mouth, a hardening of the expression of the eyes, a tightening of the knuckles. An understanding of body language is vital to the therapist, and to anyone who would understand others. The number of observers in the group ensures that no slightest expression or gesture goes unnoticed. If these can be immediately brought to the attention of the subject, he may be able to recapture the feeling that he

103

so quickly suppressed, and associate it with the situation and with its label.

Later, he may participate more actively. Instead of listening to other members giving him clues to his feelings and accepting or rejecting their identifications, he may try to observe the other members. He listens to the way in which they describe a situation, and tries to put himself in their place and imagine what their feelings were during their experience. In the beginning, he probably succeeds only in projecting his own feelings onto other people; that is to say, he ascribes to them what he himself would have felt, forgetting that they differ from him in temperament and almost certainly reacted quite differently. He need not speak his thoughts on the matter aloud. If he makes the effort to put himself in the other person's place, he also becomes able to assimilate the comments of the other members and the interpretation of the therapist, and to match these against his own. It does not matter, at this stage, whether he can see why he was right or wrong in his assessment of a feeling tone, or the reasons for an action. The most important factor is that he makes a personal effort to understand somebody else, and in so doing is able to set aside his preoccupation with his own feelings and problems. As he continues his efforts in this direction, he gradually learns to trust his judgment in matters of feelings. The more this happens, the more easily can he recapture and identify his feelings, until eventually he can allow himself to perceive an emotion at the moment it arises, to acknowledge it, and to verbal-

ize it, saying "I am angry," or "I am jealous because . . ."
Even then the reason he gives may not be the correct
one, but to have acquired the ability to verbalize his
emotions is to have jumped his first, and perhaps biggest,
hurdle.

In a therapeutic group where deep feelings are involved, communication takes place not only by means of
words and through changes of expression and posture,
but even through silences. Silences can be one of the most
expressive modes of communication, and every therapist
must know how to interpret them. For some time after
their formation, most therapeutic groups are afraid of
silences, and do their best to avoid them. Compulsive
chatter of a trivial nature, a multitude of body movements,
avoidance of glances, all betray the strain; and a young
group may easily be pushed into panic by a long silence,
unless tactfully handled by the therapist. Compulsive
chatter seldom occurs in our groups, for we deliberately
include a few individuals who have previous experience
in groups and can check it without the therapist's inter-
vention. But silences of other kinds occur. There are
silences that follow the relief of great tensions, kindly
silences filled with benevolence, silences while the members digest the interpretation of some event, perplexed or
stormy silences, explosive silences filled with anger. For
maximum communication within the group it is important
that each member identify the feeling with which a
silence is charged, even if he cannot understand the
reasons for it.

The second major goal of the therapeutic group is the solution of specific problems. Many therapists exclude the small problems of daily living from the discussions of a therapeutic group unless they very definitely lead to the exposure of attitudes and deep feelings. They make quite a rigid distinction between counseling, guidance, and psychotherapy, which is made clear in a recent article by S. R. Slavson.* He defines counseling as the evaluation and solution of a specific problem of a concrete nature. Guidance may need to explore the attitudes and feelings involved in the problem, but avoids probing into the client's unconscious motivations, and deflects his revelations as soon as threatening areas of his life are touched upon and his anxiety begins to mount. These two procedures aim at helping the client to adapt to a specific situation within the frame of reference of his existing personality. Psychotherapy, on the other hand, aims at helping the client to adapt to all situations more efficiently, by effecting changes in his personality structure; to this end both anxiety and regression are permitted to occur, and are used therapeutically.

We believe that therapy is an education in living and regard any act of daily living as holding possibilities for re-education of the client. The therapeutic groups, therefore, although primarily directed towards effecting a change of personality structure in the members, do not dismiss any question as trival or irrelevant. For example,

* Slavson, S. R. "When is a 'Therapy Group' not a Therapy Group?", *International Journal of Group Psychotherapy*, X(1), 3-15.

a mother came to the group one evening and asked for help in preparing her daughter to go to boarding-school for the first time. According to the definitions given above, this would seem to be strictly a counseling problem concerning a specific concrete question. However, in the discussion which followed, many members contributed their ideas and suggestions, which proved very valuable to the mother. One member drew on his own childhood experiences of going to boarding-school, and found that his attempt to recapture his feelings on that occasion brought into the open much repressed material which, when he discussed it with his therapist, threw a great deal of light on his current behavior patterns. What was a counseling problem for one, turned into a psychotherapeutic experience for the other.

If problems which involve deep feelings are to be discussed, the client must feel an atmosphere of warmth and respect in the group. He will not dare to expose his feelings until he is sure that he will not be judged.

An important element of this emotional climate is established outside the group. Since the formal group is but one segment of the total therapeutic process, each client has been exposed from the first day he entered therapy to a number of situations which have shown him the atmosphere of the total setting. He has experienced the warmth and friendliness, the feeling of being loved and respected, the acceptance of the other clients. He has established a relationship with me and with his therapist, and knows that we accept him. His experiences in the therapeutic community have already given him some degree of confidence and security. Now, however, he must feel the group's acceptance of him before he dares to participate. Every new member is immediately accepted by the group because the therapist has invited him to attend, but he is not always personally accepted by all of the others. The group as a whole says in effect: "We recognize in you a human being, who is entitdled to the same respect that we desire for ourselves. You are not a slave to be given orders, but a person who desires to learn how to choose values and courses of action that will bring you to maturity and responsibility for your actions. We may dislike some of your attitudes and behavior, but we do not on that account dislike you, nor reject you." Group acceptance means the recognition of the individual's potential qualities; it is their decision to make the effort to understand him, and to help him understand himself. It asks only that he will make the same effort to understand and help others.

Personal acceptance is different, however. He must earn this in his relationships with the individuals. There are certain responsibilities which group membership imposes upon the client. For example, punctuality is superficially a matter of common courtesy; to arrive late may create a disturbance, or interrupt a train of thought in a discussion that is vital to another member's growth. If we respect our fellow members, we do not do these things to them. But every action has a meaning, and says something to those who can find the meaning. Lateness, even when apparently involuntary, may have a deeper meaning. It may be that the tardy member fears that group discussion will expose a weakness of which he is still ashamed. If the chain of events leading to his lateness is examined, it is often found that he himself set up one or more of the key situations, though he may not have known at the time what he was doing. If this were passed over, he would lose an opportunity to understand more about his behavior when fear is at work on him, and perhaps an opportunity to get rid of an unnecessary fear. Other such responsibilities could be placed under a general heading called etiquette.

The most important responsibility of each group member is that of contributing, to whatever degree he is able, to the group discussions. A therapy group loses its purpose if all the members do not participate.

The individual's security is increased by the permissive atmoshere of the group. This permissiveness is seen in the removal of taboos which obtain in ordinary society, concerning morals. In almost every family violent verbal expressions of anger, bad language and discussion of sex and its problems, have been enclosed with a bright red fence, whose only gate carries a large sign "This Way to Hell." But everyone gets angry, more frequently than he likes to admit, and sexual drives which have been frustrated because of ignorance and guilt have a way of pervading and poisoning many areas of life. Only when sex can be accepted as a natural part of life, which one should neither be ashamed of nor glorify as something

109

holy, can it take its proper place. Its rightful place is in the bedroom, and it should not be allowed to usurp space in the living room and the office. Freedom to speak of it in the group robs it of its power to distort judgment, and corrects ignorance. The supportive power of the group stems largely from this very freedom; an individual may have struggled for years under a load of guilt because of a problem that he believes makes him unique. He now discovers, to his surprise and relief, that not only does the group accept the revelation of his horrendous secret calmly and without revulsion, but also that several other members have had an almost identical problem. This "universalization," the discovery that he is no longer alone, a unique monster, is one of the most powerful cohesive forces holding the group together.

A group member is often unable to uncover or to share blocked experiences, either in his private hour or in the group. The medium of psychodrama can link a minor contemporary problem to a variety of difficult early experiences. The individual can recreate these experiences in front of the group's eyes when guided by the visiting team who helped him reconstruct the actual events. This team visits each of the groups in turn, and this mode of psychotherapy acts as an extension of the usual work of the group. Following the psychodrama, the director summarizes his immediate feelings about the group member's problem and the therapist in charge of the group ties in his own personal knowledge. The group then makes its contributions to aid the subject to understand his past behavior and reveal what directions of behavior he should choose in the future.

Individual therapy sessions reveal to each one his own main behavior patterns; in the group sessions he has an additional opportunity to see behavior patterns at work in other people. The attention-seeker, the favorite, the self-appointed deputy-leader, all play their parts assiduously in the group meetings. But their roles are based on the values they acquired in childhood, and as communication improves between group members, they begin to see that the roles they have hitherto adopted are based upon mistaken premises and distorted perceptions. Each has an opportunity to try out new patterns of behavior in a perceptive group of people, whose reactions will quickly show him whether his new behavior is in accordance with the values of the therapeutic setting, and if not, the reasons for it. This is the re-educative aspect of the group sessions. In a one-to-one situation between two clients, neurotic distortions may be at work in both parties, to color their view of the real issues at stake; and this tends to leave both of them in confusion. In the group, however, the distortions are various, and tend largely to cancel out, so that the composite image of an individual or his behavior is a relatively true one. The therapist can also be relied upon to reflect a true image. For example, if a member has difficulty with authority-figures, he will probably project onto the therapist all his feelings about authority-figures. He may act towards the therapist as he did towards his father, and also use any father-like characteristics that he sees in the therapist, as an excuse to resist looking at his own behavior and changing it. But he cannot do this with a whole group of people. He can cast some of them for the roles which his parents and siblings once played, but not all of them. The other group members quickly perceive his attempts to put one of them into the position of a figure from his past. They gently and persistently point out to him each step of the operation, in such a way that he does not feel that he is being blamed. Rather, he can only feel he is being asked to look closely and see them as individuals in their own right. When he can see the members of his own group clearly as individuals, can perceive their feelings and communicate his own, then he is well on the road toward forming and maintaining mature personal relationships.

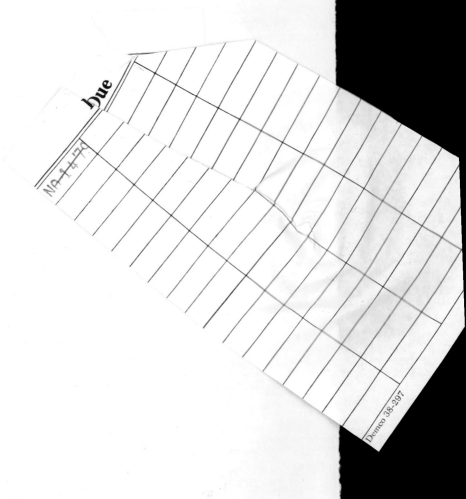